Praise for Highs and Lo\

"The current popularity of long-distance walking means that many new personal narratives have appeared in the past years. Inga Aksamit's book is a wonderful addition to these "trail tales," as she describes the 23-day trip she and her husband took along the John Muir Trail. Readers will especially be drawn to this narrative ... because it represents the experience of an "everyday" person. She and her husband set out on the JMT to challenge themselves with a much longer backcountry adventure than they'd previously completed and to experience the changing perspective one has after multiple weeks in the backcountry....Her extensive planning made her aware of all the problems that might arise - she does a superb job of weaving these into her story, one-by-one as many of the anticipated problems do materialize."

> *-Elizabeth Wenk, author of "John Muir Trail: The Essential Guide to Hiking America's Most Famous Trail"*

"As hikers we are all about preparation. We read all the trail guides, agonize over gear decisions, scrutinize every calorie we carry and look to shave ounces here and there. Particularly for hikers who are new to multi-week hikes, we show up at the trailhead with the right stuff, but not necessarily fully prepared. What about the "inside game" of a long hike? I can think of no better way to prepare oneself for the psychological rigors of the trail than by reading Ms. Aksamit's "Highs and Lows on the John Muir Trail." From unforeseen medical problems to the struggle to eat enough to the challenges of the near constant climbing, Ms. Aksamit tells her story with refreshing honesty and candor. By reading this book, potential JMT hikers will get the insights necessary to ensure that they are ready with the right attitude and expectations to ensure success."

-Raymond E. Rippel, author of "Planning your Thru-Hike of the John Muir Trail"

As a long distance backpacker myself, Aksamit's book detailing her journey on the JMT resonated strongly with me…. This book is a welcome addition to the limited selection of JMT literature….

-Michelle "Brownie" Pugh: Author of "Love at First Hike" & Appalachian Trail thru-hiker

The book is quick paced and always interesting…. Ms. Aksamit's descriptions of the scenery, of the other hikers, of her interactions, are so well written that I felt like I was right there with her.   *-B.A.M., Amazon review*

I love the descriptions of the people they met along the trip and the surprises that unfold with these fellow hikers….I found the book to be very inspiring …. The author conveys the different emotions she feels as the trip progresses, which brings the book alive.   *-L.H., Amazon review*

Inga's book contains many enjoyable trail tales and practical advice. Also she lets readers in on the emotional side of her journey, something many hikers are the least prepared for.-   *-A.J., Amazon review*

Real and inspiring!   *-R.N., Amazon review*

Highs and Lows

on the

John Muir Trail

John Muir Trail Map

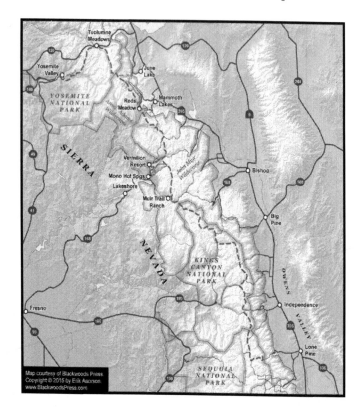

The John Muir Trail undulates 210 miles through the Sierra Nevada in California from Yosemite National Park to Mt. Whitney.

Highs and Lows

on the

John Muir Trail

Inga Aksamit

Highs and Lows on the John Muir Trail
1st Edition

ISBN 978-0-997-06180-2

Contact: www.ingasadventures.com

Photos by Inga Aksamit, unless otherwise credited

Cover design by Monique Meade, Tasty Design,
www.tastydesign.biz

Map courtesy of Blackwoods Press,
www.BlackwoodsPress.com

Published by Pacific Adventures Press

Cover photo: *Lower Cathedral Rock, Yosemite Valley*. Inga
Aksamit.
Back cover: *Echo Lakes, Desolation Valley*. Steve Mullen.

Adopt the pace of nature: her secret is patience.

-Ralph Waldo Emerson

Dedicated to Steve Mullen,
my partner in love, life and adventure.

Table of Contents

Acknowledgements

I'd like to acknowledge Molly Kurland and Norma Smith Davis for pulling more out of me than would have been possible on my own, my mother, Dorothy Aksamit, for continuing the work she has done all my life to support, encourage, inspire and edit, my father, Carroll Aksamit, for always being there for me, Crissi Langwell for corralling my commas and Laura Hovden for providing valuable input and enthusiastically participating in our adventures. And, of course, I thank Steve Mullen for being a willing accomplice and endless supporter.

Chapter 1: Fire and Lightning

I had trouble focusing as I snapped a photo of my husband standing at the marker pointing to the John Muir Trail (JMT). Steve was clad in full rain gear, grinning stoically through the drizzle. I tried to banish my foreboding thoughts to a place far away from here. The endless meadow of lush grass fringed by the sweet-smelling pine trees, the excited chatter of the fluffy-tailed gray chickarees tucking their stores away for the winter, the quiet pitter-patter of drizzle through the smoky haze—we were here on the trail, starting the longest hike of our lives. Maybe it was just the excitement of finally shouldering the packs we had labored over for so long—sorting, evaluating and debating the relative merits of each and every item contained within. No, I couldn't ignore the lightning storm at the fringes of my mind. I was getting a migraine. Like a disco ball in my head, the flashing lights of the aura slowly filled my field of vision.

Steve and I had talked extensively about a migraine strategy, but I never thought we'd have to implement it. I'd never had one in the backcountry, much less in the first ten minutes of a hike. Our pre-arranged plan was to stop, put up the tent and call it a day. But we'd only just started. To set up camp so early in our journey—in the paved parking lot of the Yosemite National Park Wilderness Center in Tuolumne Meadows, no less—seemed impractical. Besides, our permit required that we camp a minimum of four miles from the trailhead. I decided to wait and see how bad it was before sounding the alarm. Steve was striding eagerly ahead anyway. I just couldn't bear to quash his Day One/Minute One enthusiasm. Besides, as my sluggish brain recollected, Elizabeth Wenk's "John Muir Trail" guidebook had described the terrain here as the easiest and flattest of any day on our three-week trek.

I looked back toward the car, still visible in the parking lot. I considered how easy it would be to bail out. All my trepidation about the rigors of the hike came rushing toward me, drenching me with anxiety. I wondered if I had enough mojo to see this through. Did I have the stamina to make it up the passes? Would exhaustion halt me in my tracks? What if lightning struck me to the ground? What if I was overcome with altitude sickness and had to be plucked off the mountain? Would I dissolve into a mass of blubbering protoplasm, whining that I couldn't go on? Now that the migraine had settled in with all the charm of an unwanted guest, would I even make it through the first day? All I had to do was call out to Steve, tell him what was going on, climb back in the car and be whisked back to safety. I wallowed in that thought for a moment. The pull of civilization was almost too much to resist. Tears threatened to prick my eyes.

But no, I had put too much into this trip. The hours I'd spent navigating the archaic permit system, generating a collection of planning spreadsheets, training on countless steep trails and playing cheerleader to Steve's intractable ambivalence were not going to be wasted. The migraine would pass and I'd be fine tomorrow. If we gave up our permit, we were not likely to get another one. The trip would be over before it started. The path was clear. I blinked back the tears, turned away from comfort and stepped forward into the void of the unknown, inhaling the moist and slightly smoky air.

I soon caught up to Steve, who was checking the map at the first junction of two trails. I surreptitiously rummaged through my kit for my migraine medication. Was it in the red ditty bag or the gray one? And in which pocket was it in? I was sure that after days of rummaging through my packs, I would eventually know exactly where every little item was. But in the moment, the exact location of those pills escaped me. I had moved things around so much, it was a free-for-all in my pack. I finally found the medication and slipped it under my tongue, hoping it would work quickly. The aura that gives me kaleidoscope eyes was mild so far, but I had no way of knowing how severe the headache would become. I just had to wait and see.

Even with my limited vision, an effect of the aura, I could see that Lyell Canyon was dramatic in its own way. The long, grassy valley was walled in by smooth granite domes, and bisected by the gentle Tuolumne River. Scattered trees had secured improbable footholds between the overlapping slabs of rock rising from the water. The acrid odor from the inferno of the El Portal Fire, which had been burning for days, tickled my nose, and the ghostly gray clouds of billowing smoke obscured the far peaks. However, the near views were still pleasing. The wide, level trail was like a walk in the park. I had a feeling that would change when we got further into the backcountry where the terrain and views would be more dramatic.

"Can you believe this?" Steve said, gesturing toward the leaden skies. "We haven't had precipitation in a good six months in the worst drought year in history and it has to rain today?" I mumbled something about the showers being good for putting out the fire, but he said, "This little spritz isn't going to do anything to put out that conflagration, so it's just annoying." He had a point. It was 2014, the third year of a multi-year drought and the inferno, which was started by lightning, was burning through 4,689 acres of the parched forest. It was going to take more than light drizzle to quench this blaze.

When I get a migraine I don't always have the best judgment, so I waited until lunch to tell Steve about it. As I arranged our tortillas, string cheese and a cup of a gloppy concoction of corn soup on a bright blue bandana I said, "Um, I have a confession. I had a migraine this morning when we started." I handed him a cup of soup, feeling a bit chagrined that I hadn't told him right away.

"Why didn't you tell me when it first happened?" he asked.

4

"I didn't want to ruin your first day," I replied. It sounded lame, even to me.

"I thought we had a plan," he said.

"We did, but how would we have implemented it at the trailhead?" I said

At a loss for an answer, he looked at me with concern and said, "What do you want to do?"

"It's been okay since it's so flat. Let's keep going. The aura is gone and the headache isn't too bad right now. I promise I'll let you know if I start feeling sick." I was referring to the fatigue, malaise and generally yucky feeling I get after the acute migraine passes. He looked at me doubtfully, knowing there was a fifty-fifty chance that I would keep him informed. "I know I don't want to climb at all, so if the trail starts going up, let's stop," I said casually as if I had this all figured out.

"Okay. We just have a few more easy miles until we get to where I planned to stop. It's only eight miles total and we've already gone at least five. At our average of two miles an hour, that should take less than two hours." Neither of us was happy about how the first day was starting out, but there wasn't much we could do about it.

We were beginning this iconic hike, named for the famed rambler, John Muir, at the Lyell Canyon Trailhead near Tuolumne Meadows at 8,600 feet (2,621 m). We chose to commence here instead of at the official start at Happy

Isles in Yosemite Valley because it was easier to get a coveted permit. Also, that stretch of trail held no appeal since we live in California, regularly visit Yosemite National Park and have climbed Half Dome and other trails around the valley. This was a wilderness experience. Starting off with the intense hordes of tourists in the valley wasn't compatible with our vision. A side benefit was that we didn't have to pull huge elevation gain on the first day and, according to the map, it would be possible to position ourselves fairly close to Donohue Pass for a morning assault. Little did we know when we had sketched out the trip months ago that this rare flat section would benefit me so greatly.

Our plan was to hike for twenty-three days, covering 165 miles SOBO (southbound) over Kearsarge Pass to Onion Valley. This would take us through a patchwork of jurisdictions, including the Yosemite National Park, Ansel Adams Wilderness, Inyo National Forest, Devil's Postpile National Monument, Sierra National Forest, John Muir Wilderness, King's Canyon National Park and Sequoia National Park. Thankfully only one permit was required. We would also skip the last section, including Mt. Whitney, which we had hiked previously as part of the High Sierra Trail. We had a lot of backpacking experience, but this was our longest trek to date and the planning had consumed us for months. I knew the trail could throw all kinds of things at us. And yet, I had still envisioned the initial flat section to be a cinch, with blue skies, clear Sierra air, perhaps even a slight breeze kissing my cheeks. I'd pictured myself feeling

6

strong and full of energy with fresh legs. The vision had *not* involved rain gear, pack covers, gray, smoky skies or my head exploding from the inside. I guess I needed to learn from the get-go that I was not in control.

The idea that we could hike a long trail had snuck up on Steve and me. For years, we had been content with weekend or week-long backpacking trips in California, Alaska and Canada. While we hiked our little hikes, we devoured mountaineering books, living vicariously on windswept, perilous Seven Summit mountain tops we would likely never visit. When we exhausted those, we moved on to hiking narratives, repeating the Pacific Crest Trail (PCT) more times than any human could possibly replicate on two feet, never tiring of the endless recitations of the identical milestones along the 2,663-mile journey because each author brought a new perspective. We both rejected the idea of spending six months on the trail; however, the idea of a longish but not unfathomable trail became more appealing. Gradually the JMT, regarded as the most challenging as well as the most stunning part of the PCT, started to seem within reach. It still felt slightly audacious, though. Could we weekend warriors really hike that far? After testing our mettle on the seventy-two-mile High Sierra Trail, we decided we were ready for the challenge.

Now we were here and it was hard to believe that the landmarks we had read about so often were on the maps before us—never mind that I wouldn't be able to read them until the aura passed.

A few hours later, as the path steepened into carved steps, the migraine progressed to its last stage and I started feeling downright ill. My muscles were heavy and I was achy all over, sensations I was more than familiar with. I never knew whether to attribute these symptoms to the migraine itself, the medication that was supposed to abort the migraine or the medication that counteracts the nausea caused by the migraine drug. Whatever the cause, it was time to stop. The map had indicated campsites before any elevation gain. Why were we ascending?

"Are we supposed to be going up?" I asked, catching up to Steve on a switchback.

"I didn't think so." he said. "Let's fire up the GPS so we can tell exactly where we are." But this wasn't any kind of help. We could see the steep, rugged section of switchbacks without the aid of technology. "The book says there should have been some campsites back there," he said. I hadn't seen any but I didn't know what we were looking for. Were they hidden some distance off the trail or would there be an obvious campground? A big ugly "KOA Campground" sign would have been welcome at that point. However, backtracking, like the migraine plan, wasn't part of our Day One mindset. So we pressed on.

About half an hour later we found some flat tent sites in a heavily forested area near the Lyell Fork Bridge. After we set up camp Steve got a pencil, reconciled our spreadsheet against the JMT Atlas and realized that we had overshot our goal quite a bit.

"We hiked 10.7 miles today instead of the eight miles that we planned," he said proudly, "That'll really set us up nicely for the pass tomorrow."

"That would have been relatively easy if it hadn't been for my migraine," I said. *If I can do that while not being at my best, maybe this trail won't be as hard as I anticipated and it won't kick my butt,* I thought. I fantasized about us knocking out miles effortlessly, sprinting over high passes with nary a wheeze from altitude, taking side trips to nearby lakes and being fresh enough to record the day's events in my tiny notebook. I forgot for a moment that the elevation profile of the rest of the trail looked like an exaggerated Richter scale of monumental proportions, with over 45,000 feet of elevation gain and 35,000 feet of loss between all the passes. The great thing about make-believe is how soothing it is to the psyche after a tough day.

We studied the maps in the JMT Atlas, data sheet and phone app, but it was clear that they weren't quite the same and we weren't sure how to reconcile the mileage differences. Scrutinizing the almost level elevation profile of the section we had just hiked, I noticed an ever-so-slight up-tick at the end, and learned that minuscule changes on that horizontal line translated to big fluctuations underfoot. We also realized that we had likely missed the subtle signs that campsites were nearby, perhaps a faint use-trail branching off from the main track, or a slightly flattened spot in the dirt where tents had perched. I appreciated that our adjustment period was akin to moving into a new house where everything feels a bit off until you know exactly where your coffee cup is, what those sounds are on Friday morning when the garbage truck rumbles by, and where the paper gets delivered. We had everything we needed, but putting our hands on those things and interpreting environmental cues weren't yet second nature. We were in the process of finding our groove.

Earlier, we had passed a NOBO (northbound) hiker, as close to finishing his trek as we were to starting ours. He cautioned us about going over Donohue Pass so late in the day. After we emphatically reassured him that was never part of our plan, I asked, "How was it?"—"it" being our very first pass, and his last.

He had looked at me before answering, seeming to assess the best way to respond. He cocked his head to one side and with a glint in his eye, said, "There's a lot worse." Fair enough. I knew Donohue was low compared to the passes we'd encounter later on, but being the first it was looming large in my imagination. We were at such opposing sides of "trail hardness" that it wasn't even reasonable to have a shared context. I didn't pursue it, though I had many more unanswerable questions.

I pondered this exchange repeatedly as I sat by the river, waving my SteriPEN, a UV device that purifies water, through the water in my bottle. The flashing red lights were confusing me. First there had been lights in my head, now I had to sort through lights on the device. I couldn't remember what the flashing meant, but usually red meant bad and green was good. Since I had spent hours scanning owner's manuals into my Evernote app for all of our devices, I made my way back to the tent to look it up on my phone.

"Steve, you won't believe this. The SteriPEN is out of juice," I said.

"How could that be?" he asked.

"I don't know. Maybe the two shake-down trips in Tahoe used them up?" I said.

"But it's supposed to be good for something like fifty liters. We couldn't have gone through that much," he said. I tried to focus my brain on some simple calculations. Let's see, I carry two liters in my hydration bladder plus one in my Nalgene bottle...on I went, tallying all of our water breaks until I came up with roughly thirty-three liters for a weekend trip. At two trips, that was a whopping sixty-six liters. I announced my findings. We looked at each other in disbelief. "Now I can see how we're out of power," he said, not even bothering to challenge my numbers the way he usually would, he being the numbers guy. He rummaged around for the miniature multi-tool to take the SteriPEN apart.

He took the end cap off. "Shit," he said. *Uh oh*, I thought.

"What?" I asked.

"It takes two batteries," he said.

"So?" I asked.

"We only brought one extra battery for this leg," he said, looking slightly stricken. I groaned.

We discovered our first mistake. After reading at least a thousand times on the forums that we should bring a bucket of batteries for the SteriPEN, as well as supposedly checking and double checking every item, we had somehow missed the mark. Brief dithering ensued until we determined that we had at least three alternate methods of purifying water, including a small supply of iodine drops to be used in an emergency (I guess the emergency was here), boiling water on the stove (though that consumed more fuel) and a tiny bottle of bleach that I had brought for laundry. This episode left me completely wrung out, taking the last bit of reserves I had in me. I collapsed in the tent while Steve did all the camp chores.

"I feel bad that the start of our big hike was dominated by my migraine," I said over a dinner of soupy turkey tetrazzini. It was hard to feel so dragged out and wrecked on our first "easy" day, because it disconnected our shared experience. While I was hiding my problems from Steve in the morning, then just wanting to get through the afternoon and finally just wanting to sleep it off, he was full of energy and happily enjoying the initial foray.

"It's okay, there's nothing you could do to change it," he said in his usual implacable way. It drove me nuts how he could be so calm in the face of adversity, especially when I was excited about something. "It'll be a better day tomorrow after a good night's sleep. We have lots more days to enjoy the trail." I appreciated all the little things he took care of while setting up camp that night, but I knew that I had to pull my weight on a trip this long, resolving to keep the whining to a minimum.

The first day had been rough so far. We'd experienced rain, smoke, a migraine, missed calculations and spent batteries. But it was nothing we couldn't recover from. We turned in at hiker bedtime, 7:30 p.m., as shadows gathered in the dim forest. The rain started a percussive serenade against the tent walls, lulling us to sleep. I hoped that the second day would be a little smoother.

Chapter 2: First Passes

The sun was shining on our second day on the trail. The smoke had dissipated and we were full of anticipation, ready to conquer Donohue Pass. I bounded out of the tent, fully recovered from my migraine. That's the good thing about my migraines. One day I'm wrecked and then, after a good night's sleep, I'm back to normal. I bid *adieu* to the headache and looked forward to really starting my hike. We broke down camp in record time, eager to start the day.

Walking up to a small high meadow, we encountered our first mind-blowing vista: lush green grass, a stream gurgling from a placid lake, pure white egrets perched on the shore and a russet-brown doe enjoying a cool drink. Tall pine trees sheltered twittering birds. Above them, persistent snowy remnants of the once-mighty Lyell Glacier hung in the distant background. I was breathless from the beauty of it, or maybe it was the thin air. I wanted to plunk down my pack and stay awhile, but an hour into the second day was not the place to loiter—not when 11,060 foot (3352 m) Donohue Pass awaited. Looking at the glacier, I wondered if that was the pass cutting through the snowfield. The wall of granite in the distance looked massive. Its undulating ridgeline had several low depressions, but none looked inviting. I felt a sudden clutch of fear. Was I ready for this? No, the trail couldn't cut through that snow field. No one had said anything about needing crampons or ice axes. Where, then, was the route?

What little I could see of the well-defined footpath immediately before us headed toward a shorter headwall of loose talus. As we got closer, a nicely constructed trail of granite steps presented itself. How civilized! But once at the top of the steps, the dirty glacier and jumbled, rocky moraine loomed even larger. On the other side of a small valley, it looked even more daunting. I slowly scanned the escarpment.

"Do you see *anything* that looks like a trail?" I asked.

"Not where you're looking," Steve said. "It's over that way." He pointed at the hairpin turn that led toward a much more benign scene, away from the glacier. Relieved, I looked at the long, lazy switchbacks that snaked through the monotonous gray rock.

It turned out to be a good training pass, tough enough to make us breathe hard, but not discouraging. We established what would become our "pass pattern"— stopping for a photo, having a snack and sharing stories with others hanging around the pass. We talked briefly with a few people, agreeing that it was a challenge and that the view of Lyell Canyon was worth it. We exchanged cameras with another couple and took pictures of each other by the pond at the top with jutting peaks in the background.

Passes are funny. They are the absence of height, and crossing over them is the opposite of peak bagging, which is summiting the tallest feature. A pass is the easiest way over a ridge. Yet there's a feeling of accomplishment, somewhat dampened by looking around and seeing plenty of higher places. So it was with Donohue, a bit anticlimactic, but a small triumph nonetheless.

Before heading down, we took one last look at the flat expanse of Lyell Canyon, where we walked the day before. Billowing white pyrocumulus clouds from the fire rose in the distance, competing for attention with the granite domes that formed the skyline. That was it for Yosemite. We had spent less than twenty-four hours there and we were already out the other side. We turned our attention to the striking Ritter Range and spikey Minarets poking into the blue sky in Inyo National Forest. A grassy meadow awaited our descent, surrounded by walls of light gray granite.

The boggy terrain just under the pass was criss-crossed with many wildflower-bordered streams linking shallow ponds. The trail was a deep groove worn several inches lower than the surrounding terrain. No need to pull out a map here. In fact, the track was as obvious as a well-signed freeway, complete with off-ramps to side trails at well-marked junctions. With our heads down, looking at the rut to avoid obstacles, we strode down the mountain.

We barely remembered to look up to watch the changing panorama of peaks, but when we did, we could see the sky filling with smoke. The clear blue skies we had enjoyed in the morning were gradually obliterated. Snowflakes of ash drifted down from the sky. We tried to figure out how the canyons were funneling smoke because it seemed to be getting worse instead of better, even as we put more distance between us and Yosemite and the El Portal fire.

After an afternoon of comfortable walking, we set up camp in a secluded spot under the trees beside Rush Creek. I shuffled through our food stores, counting how many more days before our first re-supply at the pack station at Red's Meadow—three more. That would make five days for this stretch, a normal backpacking trip. We would have eighteen more after we picked up our resupply box of food. The number seemed enormous. That's when I understood, at a deeper, more visceral level, how long this hike really was. I knew it was a short time compared to PCTers, who spend five or six months on the Pacific Crest Trail. But for me, twenty-three days in the wilderness sounded like a very long time. The spreadsheets, mileage goals and meal plans we had labored over at home had somehow become more abstract as the planning became more concrete. In my kitchen, the hike had turned into an intellectual exercise more than a physical endeavor. Two solid days on the trail and getting over our first pass felt satisfying, but the reality that many more days and higher passes lay before us threatened to overwhelm me. I pulled myself back from the abyss. *Just take things one day at a time,* I reminded myself. I pulled up the guidebook on my phone and read about what was to come tomorrow—that's all I needed to focus on for now. The rest would take care of itself.

Busying myself getting dinner together, I found that the familiar routine helped to center me. When I had planned our food for the trip, I decided to alternate between freeze-dried Mountain House packaged meals and home-dehydrated dinners to give us a lot of variety. I dug around in our bear barrel, a hard-sided plastic canister designed to keep prying paws out of our food supply, and found my home-laminated meal plan. I had covered the paper printout with wide strips of packing tape on both sides to make it reasonably waterproof. Our dinner menu for today featured Asian stir-fry served over brown rice. At home, I had sautéed chicken and veggies in an Asian sauce, then spread it on round trays in the dehydrator for eight hours. By the time it was ready to be vacuum sealed in a bag, it was dry and crunchy. I had also cooked brown rice in my rice steamer, then dehydrated it for six hours. It seemed silly to take a dry product, cook it in water, then dry it again, but the process saves both fuel and time to soak it in water on the trail rather than having to maintain a simmer for twenty minutes.

At the campsite, I poured hot water into one freezer bag with the dehydrated pre-cooked rice, and into another one with the homemade stir-fried chicken and veggies. Adding some Sriracha sauce that I had dried to pliable leather, I mushed it around to mix it in. I slipped both bags into a warmer, similar to a tea cozy, that we had made from reflective insulating material duct-taped together. Twenty minutes later we would have a savory meal. I passed the time sitting on a log near our camp and communed with a deer who wandered into the clearing. We just looked at each other for a long moment. Then he went about his business, bending his head down to munch on his dinner of presumably tasty leaves while I waited for mine.

I contemplated how it was that we got here, not just on the trail, but how our lives became intertwined. It had taken me a long time to find Steve. I didn't know what I was looking for, but I was quite sure I hadn't found it after dating a series of doctors who had no time for adventure, musicians who only cared about their art and outdoorsmen who didn't care enough about making a living. Skiing was my passion and though Steve and I skied together with a group of friends who were advancing through intensive ski clinics, it took a couple of years before we noticed each other. Suddenly I recognized him. He was the reliable guy with a good job who still experienced life to the fullest. What he lacked in grace he made up for with gusto as he rocketed down the slopes without fear. The rest of us learned to put him first, not only to lead the way but to avoid the terror that came with knowing there was a good chance he was cartwheeling behind us, threatening to behead us with his jet-propelled skis.

He lived in Tahoe and I lived in the San Francisco Bay Area so we only saw each other sporadically during the winter. I didn't think anything would come of our fledgling romance as I was relocating from San Francisco to Seattle to work as a nursing director at the world-renowned Fred Hutchinson Cancer Research Center. He surprised me, though, saying, "I've never lived in a city. That might be cool." Off we went to my final interview. While I climbed the steep incline to Pill Hill to meet with my future boss he explored the city and that evening we agreed that we were both moving. When he pulled out a glittering ring over flutes of sparkling wine in the Space Needle and proposed marriage, our future together was sealed.

Together we sought out new adventures, throwing ourselves into exciting sports such as mountain biking, kayaking and rock climbing and more sedate activities like gardening and exploring the great Northwest with equal gusto. Getting Steve to take up backpacking again took a few years of coaxing. He had "been there, done that." I was thrilled when he finally agreed to go for one night only. We packed up a motley collection of my bulky car camping gear and his ancient Boy Scout kit. With cups, pads and sleeping bags hanging off of our too-small backpacks like a gangly Christmas tree we clanked up a steep trail near our cabin in Tahoe.

That night, with moonlight streaming through the pine boughs Steve sat back staring at the hypnotic flames of the campfire in the Granite Chief Wilderness. "This is pretty nice," he said. "You know, if we got new packs and sleeping bags we probably wouldn't need much more equipment." I held my breath, waiting for him to go on. "Maybe we could even hike the Chilkoot Trail in Alaska. I'd love to do that." I didn't care which trail we did, but I jumped in enthusiastically.

"You did love all that Klondike gold rush history up there, didn't you? Just think about it. We could follow in the footsteps of the prospectors. I'll bet there are even artifacts still there."

"Now that would be a reason for me to take up backpacking again," said Steve. And so it was done. We became backpackers together from that moment, acquiring better gear, bringing my skills up to snuff while updating his and we've been going strong ever since, our contrary yin and yang forces often balancing each other. I throw an idea out, he nixes it, I throw it out again and he absentmindedly agrees. Before he can change his mind I put the wheels in motion and then he fully engages. Well, eventually he engages, after a period of backpedaling, asking silly questions such as, "Why again are we doing this?" Just when I get exasperated that he's not on board, he'll suddenly commit, laying out the plan in meticulous detail on spreadsheets. He'll pore over maps, elevation profiles, water sources and legal campsite locations to put together a giant puzzle to keep us within our limits of comfortable hiking.

We both like to cook at home, but I fell into the role of commissary organizer while he took care of the cooking kit. I started off strong, initially bringing a skillet to make complicated multi-part meals. I gradually simplified our menu to the freezer-bag cooking method we were using tonight. The minimal preparation and cleanup was appealing and the purchase of a home dehydrator had opened up a whole new world of pre-assembled recipes that greatly expanded our trail diet. Steve embarked on a typical backpacker path of stove acquisition, regularly falling for the latest in lightweight technology and fuel efficiency. The rest of the kit got lighter, too, with discarded cups, cutlery and plates filling a box of equipment relegated to car camping, which we never did. Along with the stove, he now carried just two bowls, two folding spoons and two insulated cups.

I returned to my kitchen area and opened the freezer bag, reassuringly heavy and warm in my hands, releasing an appetizing aroma of soy sauce and exotic spices that wafted through our campsite.

"Dinner's ready," I called out to Steve, who had been sitting in his camp chair reading, as I squeezed the food into our plastic bowls. We unfolded the long handles of our spoons and dug in. "Mmmmm," I said, relishing the complex burst of flavors and bite of the hot sauce. "That's a big improvement over the soup." The lentil soup that I had enjoyed on previous trips didn't cut it on this trip. It had tasted bland, grainy and thin at lunch, almost making me gag.

"That was okay. I didn't mind it," Steve said. He had never been one to be fussy about food. But for me, the altitude always messes with my appetite so I'm more sensitive to aromas and textures that aren't quite right.

"This is tasty, though," he continued. "And there's a lot of it. I think your homemade meals are more robust than the store-bought ones." That made me happy since the home dehydrator was a new venture and I hadn't been sure how the meals would go over with Steve. We went to bed that night with warm, full bellies.

The Minarets, our constant companions for the next couple of days, were clearly etched against the Windex-blue sky in the morning. Smoke again softened the sharp sawtooth edges by afternoon. Island Pass, at 10,200 feet (3108 m) barely qualified as a pass because the elevation gain was so minimal and the ascent so gradual. However, I rejoiced to have a second one under our belts. The outsized reward for such a trifling effort was a stunning view. Tiny Island Lake posed as a postcard from the Alps, framed by the graceful glacier-laden Banner Peak, jutting toward the heavens. Masses of nearby blue and white lupine, scarlet paintbrush and sunny yellow Sierra butterweed swayed in a gentle breeze. The stunted pine trees warmed their limbs in the sun, the harsh winter behind them. Throwing my pack down I sprinted toward the lake, arms outstretched, wanting to embrace the whole of it in my heart forever. I ran back to Steve, the established time keeper. "Can we stay for a break? I know we just had one but this is too magical to pass up," I said.

"Sure. We can do anything we want," he said, sounding uncharacteristically affable. Usually he's focused on keeping us on track to make sure we don't dally too much. Since he put the plan together, he's the one who keeps us on some sort of schedule. I'd love to wander freely through the woods, ambling around each pretty lake photographing the cornucopia of colors provided by all the tiny wildflowers that spring from the earth. But I'm also the one who'll be whining when we're still trudging down the trail at dusk.

I darted back to the lake. "Come here, you have to see. Bring the camera. Take a picture, quickly," I said, too overcome with the beauty to slow down.

"Hold on just a minute. It's not going anywhere," he said with a laugh. "Come and get your pack, and let's sit down for a proper break."

"I can't. It's too beautiful. I just have to sit here and lap it up," I said, my heart swelling with pure rapture. "Can't you just see a little one-room cabin here with a little puff of smoke coming out of it before John Muir ever came on the scene? Just a little cabin in the woods, right here for us. Oh, I want to live here and never go anywhere else, ever again." He laughed again. He'd heard me say that I want to live somewhere different just about everywhere we go. He brought my pack to me.

Once Steve pried me from Island Pass, we got back on the trail. But the magnificent views just kept coming. Thousand Island Lake soon appeared on the horizon and sported a slightly different view of Banner Peak. This lake was much larger, the blue water dotted with many small, rocky islands. Often named as one of the most scenic places on the trail, it was striking, but lacked the intimacy that made the little lake at Island Pass so appealing to me. Gems came fast and furiously as we passed Emerald Lake, Ruby Lake and Garnet Lake in rapid succession.

We cleared a big hill that felt more like a pass with its gradual incline, and were rewarded at the end with an enchanted lodgepole pine forest, often referred to as *tamarack* in the west. Sun filtered through the smoky air and trees throwing pools of ghostly golden light on the trail next to slabs of dove gray granite. Symmetrical geometric shapes lined the rock with fascinating precision—a perfect square here, and an isosceles triangle there. The straight lines intersected like a stone road map, pointing back to the time when massive geologic forces shaped this land. The forest was open here, possessing plenty of room between the tall trees. One could feel free to ramble cross-country, like Muir did, if miles didn't have to be made. My untethered mind wandered, ruminating about how wonderful it would be to dwell in this perfect woodland. I caught up to Steve, prattling on about my musings.

"I love tamarack trees," I said in a sing-song voice. "They're so friendly and welcoming, with plenty of room for all. It's perfect for sheltering gentle forest creatures. If I were creating a forest for Bambi, I'd use this one with soft spongy paths, green meadows and babbling brooks full of glistening rainbow trout. What are you thinking about?"

With nary a pause he said, "I designed the Tahoe kitchen in my head, then the summer kitchen, then the office bathroom and now I'm working on a plan for the office to become a studio rental."

"Really?" I was nonplussed, but I caught myself before I said anything more. We each had our own way of enjoying the long, peaceful stretches in the woods, and we were different people, each in our own Venus and Mars worlds. "That's great. You're getting a lot done while I'm lost in whimsy, dreaming about fairy tales."

At the end of every day Steve would pull out our planning spreadsheet and note our mileage, making sure that we stayed roughly on track, even if we didn't adhere exactly to the plan. And every day I'd ask how many miles we hiked, always thinking that we had exceeded our first day's achievement. That conversation pretty much played out in some form almost every night.

"How many miles today?" I asked.

"Let's see, today we hiked all of 6.6 miles," Steve said, citing a ridiculously low number.

"Huh?" I said. "That's embarrassing."

"Why?" he said. "We planned easy days on this first section so we could acclimate to the altitude and not kill ourselves on the first couple of passes."

"I know. I remember that. But somehow I reasoned that a six-mile day would feel really short, more like a half-day. I thought I'd be lively, scampering around exploring side trails near our campsite. Not collapsed in the tent at four o'clock, napping," I said. "Why do I feel so wiped out?"

"Uh, because we're going over 11,000-foot passes, and we're gaining and losing 4,000 feet of elevation every day," he said, ever the logical one.

"Humph," I said in mild disgust.

That night I read through the guidebook and remembered a trip report I had in my Kindle. It was an account of a new speed record by Ralph Burgess from a thread on the JMT Yahoo Group. "Hey Steve, did you hear about that guy, Ralph, who set the solo unsupported SOBO speed record?" I asked.

"Yeah, I saw something about it. But we were so busy the last couple of days that I didn't really pay attention," he said.

"I copied his account into my Kindle. Want to read it?" I asked.

"Sure," he said and quickly scanned through it with the application on my phone, saying simply, "That's pretty interesting," in that tone he uses to indicate he sort of absorbed it but wasn't curious to learn more. I read through it again, impressed with Ralph's achievement. I still didn't have enough familiarity with the trail to know where the landmarks were. However, it was very apparent that our pace was at the opposite end of the speed spectrum. Our piddling six- to ten-mile days were nothing compared to

Ralph's forty-mile (or more) days. We were hiking our own hike (HYOH), finding that to be challenging and satisfying enough.

We had camped at Rush Creek, an unnamed lake and Johnson's Meadow. After three nights of tenting in solitude, we couldn't help wondering where the famous crowds were on this popular trail. We did pass a few other backpackers, many looking like they were out for two- or three-night trips. But these encounters rarely elicited more than brief greetings as we passed each other by. Maybe the JMT was too short to have the kind of trail camaraderie I'd read in narratives about the PCT and other long trails. Or maybe everyone was using their energy to adjust to the trail and the altitude, and they didn't have anything left over for social interaction.

"I thought we would see more people on the trail, didn't you?" I said.

"Yeah, I guess I did. People talk about it being like a highway so I was expecting to be camping with groups of people every night and to see more people on the trail," said Steve.

"We've seen a few clumps of people here and there but who would have thought that we'd camp as much as we have by ourselves," I said.

"It's just as well. I don't need to be with a bunch of yahoos every minute," said Steve.

"True. It's hard to tell who is thru-hiking and who is out for the weekend. I had hoped we'd meet some people from the Yahoo and Facebook groups," I said.

Soon we started seeing trail runners, day-hikers and dogs, which was a little disorienting. We realized we were already brushing civilization again as we approached Red's Meadow, the site of our first resupply. It seemed too soon as if we hadn't been out long enough.

Before I figured out exactly where we were, I decided to start asking people what they were up to. I asked one hiker without a pack if he was camped out here somewhere. He said, dismissively, "No, I live here." *Right here?* I wondered. *In Inyo National Forest?* As I tried to detach myself from his adorable Australian Shepard, Cody, who kept getting tangled up between my legs, I conjured up a vision of a hermit house in a giant tree stump with a little chimney and a big pot of savory squirrel stew. I must have looked puzzled because he then added, "In Mammoth." Oh, okay, that makes more sense, a real town with subdivisions and well-stocked grocery stores. "I'm just walking the dog, our regular fifteen-mile walk." *That's some dog walk.* Later, I pieced together that day-hikers can take a shuttle to Agnew Meadows, walk on a trail to Red's and then pick up the shuttle again from a road. We were that close to the real world.

As I looked back on the past few days, every lapis lake, cozy campsite and high pass was sharply etched in my memory. Yet nothing of consequence stood out. The four days were a blur of minor adjustments and uneventful hiking, a welcome change from the first day. The migraine was a distant memory, our blend of water purification methods had held out, we were adjusting to the altitude and lightning had not struck us to the ground. So far, so good. However, the smoke was worse and I hoped we wouldn't be dogged by it the whole trip.

So far we had already covered thirty-seven miles in four and a half days, including two passes. Our first section, from Tuolumne Meadows to Red's Meadow, was all about settling in and getting accustomed to the nuances of our guidebooks and maps. It sure wasn't Ralph's pace, but the relaxed tempo was allowing us time to acclimate and ease into the trail. I looked forward to the next part as we became more trail-hardened. We would also have company to look forward to when our teenaged godson, Chase, and his mom, Laura, would join us for a few days of the hike at Red's Meadow.

Chapter 3: Red's Meadow

I heard soft footfalls in the fine dirt. "Is this the way to Red's?" a young man asked as he came up behind me. I looked back at a stout young man with a baby face framed incongruously by a silky full beard, a red bandanna tied around his head to hold his light brown hair back. He had a ready smile. He was followed closely by his companion, a fresh-faced fellow with a slim build. It was the first of many rapid-fire questions from Baby Face.

"Yes, as far as I know," I replied.

"Are you hiking the JMT?" he asked.

"Yes, we are. How about you?" I said.

"Yep. Isn't it beautiful? Sometimes I'm overcome with emotion. I almost want to cry," he said.

"It's stunning," I agreed, moved that this sensitive young man was so in touch with his feelings.

"We don't have anything like this where we live in Chicago," he continued without a pause.

"Wow, that's pretty far away," I said.

"We've only been backpacking once to get ready for this trip. I've been getting in shape and I've lost a bunch of weight. I'll probably lose more here," he said, ricocheting from one topic to another.

"Good for you. This trail is a big one, considering that it's only your second trip," I said, trying to process the flow of disparate facts coming at me.

"Yeah, I guess we bit off the big one. We've been trying to learn as much as we can, and bought all this gear this summer," he said. Their attire and gear looked like any other distance hiker, so they did a good job.

"My brother has done some backpacking and he lives in California. He's been giving me advice and living vicariously through our adventure," said his reserved buddy. Ah, that explained the quality gear.

This quick exchange was the most we had spoken to anyone on the trail. It buoyed my spirits to feel in sync with people I had just met, connecting with others who felt the beauty of the trail so deeply. Baby Face, also known as Kevin, and Danny, the quiet one, were the first people I met where I felt like I was experiencing the social aspect of life on the trail. I had no doubt that the hubris and strength of youth would carry them right to the top of Mt. Whitney. Kevin's effervescence and Danny's attentiveness would surely attract a boatload of trail friends along the way.

"We'll get out of your way," I said, pulling over to the side of the trail just as we broke out of the forest into an idyllic open meadow of green grass with a stream running through it. The only thing that marred this bucolic scene was the persistent cloud cover mixed with smoke. "Fast hikers," I called out to Steve. Steve and I usually called out to each other to move to the side when we could sense people gaining on us since most of the younger hikers were much faster than we were. I was okay with being slower, "hike your own hike" and all that. At least I thought I was okay with that. It wasn't that I minded being slower than the younger kids. It was just disappointing because I had assumed my pace would be a little brisker by now.

"Speed demons, huh," said Steve, smiling at the young men.

"Oh no, we're in no hurry and we've heard it's confusing around here," said Danny. They did step ahead of us, but we ended up continuing our conversation and navigated around the confusing maze of trails together. I had a detailed map of the area in my phone, but it inconveniently died after four days without a charge.

Steve pulled out his trail atlas and the three of them bent their heads over the map pointing this way and that while I hung back letting them do their thing. I wandered over to a bridge and found a sign. They were having so much fun I almost hated to break up the map-fest, but I said, "Hey, guys, the sign says this way to Devils Postpile National Monument. I don't think we need a map." They looked up but didn't move and Steve didn't put the map away.

"Okay, we'll be right there," said Steve. They went back to the map for a few minutes and then gave up, walking over to the bridge. "I think it's that way," I said, pointing in the direction of the arrow. We could see people coming from the opposite direction on a wide, level trail that clearly saw more foot traffic than the single track we had just come through.

We walked to the popular Postpile together, forming a worn-looking group. Our unwashed bodies contrasted mightily with the SoCal tourists on day hikes from Mammoth, with their bright, colorful spandex and scrubbed faces. The fashion styles between Northern California and Southern California were noticeable, even out here. Tipping our heads back, we snapped pictures of the sixty-foot-high Postpile, a geologic formation resulting from lava that cooled in regular hexagonal columns 80,000 to 100,000 years ago, and admired nature's handiwork for a brief moment. The boys were anxious to keep moving as they had a schedule to keep, planning to get their resupply and then hiking on in the afternoon. Their admirable plan differed from our strategy to take a zero day (hiking zero miles) with two nights at Red's Meadow, in deference to our "mature" bodies that needed extra rest.

We made our way to Red's Meadow Resort by following signs and asking passersby. Presently the pine scent of the forest mixed with an inoffensive barnyard odor and we knew we were close. After passing horse corrals, the first building we saw was the store, a long wooden structure fronted by a low wall of smooth, rounded river rocks. A large, hand-painted map by the entrance illustrated the network of trails in the area while an American flag waved in the gentle breeze. The rustic backcountry camp might have stretched the traditional definition of "resort." However, after being in the backcountry for a few days, the rough cabins, corrals, Mule House Café, store, communal shower house and laundromat clustered together spelled pure luxury, earning every bit of the resort moniker. Unfortunately for us, I had been under some delusion that we would be so enthralled with the trail that we would want to eschew such comforts and we had no reservations. I didn't even have to ask if there were any openings because I could hear every single person before me ask about availability as I waited in line at the store to pick up our resupply boxes. There were none.

"What's the name on your box?" the clerk at the store asked.

"Mullen. Steve Mullen," I responded.

She disappeared into a large storeroom at the back of the store and I could see her looking for our box among stacks and stacks of boxes piled high. She returned with a small box. I brought the box to Steve, who was sitting outside on a bench.
"Here it is. Isn't this exciting?" I said.

"I guess. It's only food. It's not like there's any big surprises in there. He always has a more logical view of life. I started taking the tape off.

"It seems so small. Did we really get all that food in this little box?" I said.

"I guess. If that's our box, we must have," said Steve. I paused.

"Wait a minute, I guess I should double check," I said, tipping the box so I could read the label. "John Mullen! This isn't our box."

"Better go get ours," said Steve, reclining on his bench. I went back in the store, coming back a few minutes later with a larger box.

"That's more like it," said Steve.

I tore into our box just as Kevin and Danny came up with theirs. It was as if we hadn't seen the packages in months, rather than the two-week interval since we had packed them up and mailed them. Bags of rice, pasta and couscous tumbled out, as well as dehydrated sauces, energy bars, drink powders, soup mixes, tortillas and breakfast cereal. We exclaimed over each other's resupply treats, such as Snickers bars for the boys and Jelly Belly jelly beans for me. We commiserated over the needed supplies we couldn't find in the store, such as batteries and water purification drops. We went in and out of the store several times just to make sure they didn't have what we wanted.

"Did you find any purification drops?" I asked Kevin.

"No, they're out. But the woman in the store was so nice to me. She offered to give me bleach. She said that's what the PCT hikers use. But I need to find a small container."

"I guess if bleach is good enough for PCTers, it's good enough for JMTers," I said.

We searched through the store one more time, looking at the toiletry section, but couldn't find what he needed. We found lures and tackle, coolers of cold beer and soft drinks, boxes of apples, oranges, plums and bananas, yogurt, cheese, deli meats, pancake mix and potato chips, but no dropper bottles. I remembered the eye drop bottle I had purchased the day before we started when I thought our eyes might burn from the smoke of the forest fires.

"You can have my Visine bottle. I haven't needed it," I said.

"Really? Thank you so much. I can't believe how helpful everyone is," said Kevin. Problem solved. I watched the patient folks at Red's figure out workarounds over and over, handing out large, black garbage bags to a group of Japanese hikers when they had run out of ponchos after the drizzle started and finding the right cords to help foreign visitors of all stripes charge their electronics, using sign language when language barriers prevented communication.

We ate BLTs (fresh juicy tomatoes! crunchy bacon! crisp lettuce!) and burgers with creamy potato salad and deliciously salty chips with Kevin and Danny, swapping stories about trails. Even though their backpacking experience was limited, they already had a good bear story. It was the first night of the hike at the hiker campground at Little Yosemite Valley. After setting their packs down to scout out a spot, they turned around just in time to see a large black bear strolling off with Danny's pack. They, and a group of hikers, ran after the bear yelling and screaming, scaring him enough that he dropped the pack. It was covered in bear saliva, so Danny's new pack was properly christened and he acquired the trail name Bear Slobber. The bears in Yosemite are smart. They've learned that the bear canisters are hard to get into, but that sometimes they can find snacks people have left in their packs.

Steve came alive after this exchange, regaling the boys with some of our previous wilderness adventures. He doesn't crave social interaction like I do but he does like people and he warmed up quickly to these beguiling young men. They asked lots of questions, which just got him going more. Pretty soon he had exhausted our repertoire of backcountry stories and moved on to international travel. Finally, they realized they needed to get back on the trail and took off, exchanging emails with us and promising to check in after the trip.

Resigned to staying in the nearby Forest Service car-camping campground instead of a cabin, we decided to put it off as long as possible, hanging out at the picnic tables between the store and café until mid-afternoon. We were amazed to see a pickup truck pull up to the back of the store loaded with more hiker boxes. They had made a run into the post office at Mammoth. The storeroom looked full but somehow, one by one, the boxes were stowed away. It gave us a good appreciation for the enormous service they provide for thru-hikers.

We finally settled in, trudging the 0.2 miles (that felt like at least two miles) to the Red's Meadow Forest Service campground. After wandering around the campground on tired feet, we finally found the host who directed us to the backpackers' campsite, basically one campsite divided into three tiny sections. Each was equipped with a bear-proof box and picnic table. The scene was dreary, with the omnipresent smoke and rain showers, so we just erected the tent under a protective tree, threw our gear inside and caught the shuttle to the town of Mammoth. I have to admit that it felt good to be transported without having to use my legs. The shuttle driver entertained us with stories about the red-bearded "Red" Sotcher, who homesteaded here in 1879. That explained why everything in the area is named "Red's," including the resort and campground.

"Do you have any CR123 batteries?" I asked the clerk at Mammoth Mountaineering.

"I'm pretty sure we do," she said, rummaging through the row of batteries hanging on the wall. I held my breath, hoping the uncommon batteries were there. Maybe the third time was a charm, being as this was the third store we visited after taking three shuttles.

"I'm so sorry." My heart sank. "We only have an eight-pack." My heart sang.

"We'll take them," I said, pouncing on the package. "Maybe even two packs."

"Let's not get carried away," Steve said. "Batteries are heavy." Always the voice of reason, we compromised by adding some chlorine drops as a backup to all our other backups.

"Are you doing the John Muir Trail?" the clerk asked.

"Yes, we are. Do we smell or something?" I asked.

"No," she laughed. "But you get a ten percent JMT discount."

"Sweet. Mammoth Mountaineering is my favorite store in this entire town," I said happily.

The store was across the street from the motel where we had dropped off a box of clean clothes a week before. Though they were for when we finished the trail, it was almost too tempting to think we could just walk over there, change clothes and go home. I found it jarring to mingle among tourists attending a big music festival in town, and although the cafés looked tempting, I just wanted to get back to Red's Meadow. I knew if I attempted a rest day at Mammoth I'd never get back on the trail.

"Do you want to eat here? I see they have pizza," I said to my pie-loving husband. I was willing to defer to his hunger for real food even though I had no desire to mingle with the tourists.

"No, it's too much being here with all these people. Let's just go back to Red's," he said.

"Fine by me. This scene is a bit much for me, too," I replied, relieved. It was nice to know we were in sync.

We stood at the shuttle stop across the street from the store and hopped on the next shuttle.

"They sure make it easy to get around town with these free shuttles," I said to Steve.

"Yeah, I wish Tahoe had something like this," he said.

"We should be back in less than an hour," I said glancing down at my watch. All of a sudden I realized we were turning left instead of right. "Where are we going?" I said.

"I don't know. Weren't we supposed to turn right there to get to the ski area?" said Steve. The doors opened and everyone got off, discharged into a swirling mass of people swarming the bus.

"Oh, no. This is the music festival. Aaargh. I think we have to get off. This must be an event shuttle."

"Ugh," said Steve. We pushed our way out of the bus, finding ourselves in the midst of crowds of people going in every direction, in portapotty lines, food lines, bus lines and other lines that I couldn't figure out. Sensory overload was immediate and I started making unfocused movements trying to determine how to proceed.

"Wow, there are a lot of people here. This must be special, but it's too much. Don't you think?" I said, hoping that he agreed.

"Yes, it's way too much. Too many people. Let's get out of here," said Steve.

"Should we wait for the shuttle going in the other direction?" I said.

"No, let's just walk to the corner and make sure we get on the right shuttle this time," said Steve.

"All the way up there?" I said, eyeing the thousand or so feet to the corner. He laughed.

"You just walked from Yosemite to Mammoth. I think you can walk a block," said Steve.

"You're right. Let's go," I said, against the protests of my fatigued legs.

We boarded the correct shuttle and returned to our campsite by late afternoon but didn't spend much time there except to sleep. We found the combination of drizzle and haze from the nearby fire to be unappetizing. The folks who run Red's Meadow Resort had told us that the smoke was from an entirely different fire than the one we knew about in Yosemite. The smoke we had been experiencing the last couple of days, when we had noticed that it seemed to be getting worse instead of better, was from the human-caused French Fire.

We spent most of our time at the resort instead of the campground. Our entertainment was the endless stream of hikers coming through. The general routine we observed was for hikers to wander in, slightly dazed at confronting even this slight modicum of civilization, request their box from the cashier at the store, sort through their resupply and dump discards in the hiker barrels.

A hot shower with soap, shampoo and cream rinse was glorious. Enveloped in steam, I wanted the warm water to course over me forever, washing away the layers of grime that had already built up. But sadly, the flow was timed. Once we were clean, we joined a throng of oddly dressed people. Many were attempting to wash every single item of clothing they had with them in the laundry so the choices of how to cover their bodies in public were amusing. We wore our rain gear, but one young man strolled around wearing nothing but his sleeping bag, conveniently equipped with arm and leg holes. Between laundry cycles I checked my electronics charging at an outlet in the café, cruised by the hiker barrel regularly to see if there was anything yummy to snack on and circulated through the store assessing whether you could really resupply there. The answer was yes, especially for the undiscriminating hiker. There were freeze-dried Mountain House dinners, boxes of Minute Rice, packages of ramen, tortillas, string cheese and more.

Steve read books on his Kindle and plotted out our next section of the hike when Chase and Laura would be with us. Their trip had been up in the air for months after Laura had a ski accident in March, requiring surgery. Fifteen-year-old Chase liked to backpack with us but preferred the camping part more than the walking part. "I'm worried about tomorrow. We'll be fine because we're acclimated to the altitude and we're getting trail hardened, but ten miles is a lot for Laura and Chase just coming from sea level. And we don't know how her knee will do. How long has it been since her surgery?" he said.

"About five months. She says she's been hiking ten miles, but that's without a pack," I responded.

"That's not much time, even for someone as tough as Laura. I don't know that Chase has ever hiked ten miles with a backpack on. I've been thinking that if we could hike just a few miles tomorrow it would make the next day so much easier for all of us," he said.

"But tomorrow is our zero day," I said, clinging to my treasured day off. Back and forth we went until he convinced me that the first three miles out of Red's was easy. Laura, who grew up among the hardy individualists who characterize the "live free or die" state of New Hampshire, was the most determined person we knew. If she had to go from sea level to 10,000 feet and hike forever she'd do it without complaint even with a limp, but Chase would certainly squawk. I really did want Laura and Chase to enjoy their short time with us and not feel like it was a death march. I sent a text to Laura asking if they could get to Mammoth early enough to hike for a couple of hours and she was immediately on board. She said they would try to get an early start the next morning. So much for my zero day.

Eating all of our meals at the Mule House Café, we found the food to be tasty, filling, reasonably priced and superior to freeze-dried in every possible way. That evening we enjoyed grilled salmon, potatoes and salad with the perfect wine, a crisp and refreshing Happy Camper Chardonnay. The two waiters were a married couple who chatted it up with us and other hikers. Somehow they maintained a lively interest in the exact same stories day after day as thru-hikers and tourists passed through.

I noticed that people talked among themselves but there wasn't much chatter between groups. Most trekkers had only been hiking a few days and were still in a learning mode, as were we. I wondered if people would open up more as the trail went on, my thoughts migrating toward Kevin and Danny with hopes they were having fun. We had had less social contact than expected but I knew that was about to change with the arrival of Chase and Laura tomorrow.

We headed back to the campground and turned in early. I needed my beauty sleep, especially if I was only going to get a nero (nearly zero miles) day instead of a full zero day.

Chapter 4: Fish Creek

The day started off with a volley of texts from Laura and Chase alerting us to their progress. We had a long day of anticipation at the Mule House Café, where we had regular feedings every two hours to stock up in advance of the next section of hiking. An egg breakfast, ice cream, pie, potato chips, sandwiches and other "real" food slid down easily. Every 15 minutes Steve said, "Have you heard anything from Laura?" and I'd check my phone to give him a status update. He was anxious to get on the trail. We checked and rechecked our bags, ate a little more, surveyed the hiker barrels and cruised through the store for the hundredth time. My electronics were taking forever to charge so I checked those often as well. "Are they almost here?" asked Steve again.

Chase and Laura finally stepped off the shuttle at 5 p.m. Chase looked even taller than the last time we saw him, becoming more of a beanpole as he towered over Laura. Her long, golden hair was streaked with gray, but she still looked young and fit with muscular legs extending from her hiking shorts. All those triathlons and full moon swims in 50-degree San Francisco Bay had toned her so much that even the last five months of enforced inactivity after her knee surgery didn't show. Although they had had a dawn start to their day and protracted hours of driving from the San Francisco Bay Area, they were raring to go and we were beyond ready. After hugs and a quick review of the map mural on the side of the store to show them our route, we took off. Our plan was to get to Red Cones that night, just a few miles away. We had a spring in our step, anticipating their company over the next three days.

Wenk had this to say about the next section of her guidebook: "To many, the next section is among the most monotonous of the JMT," which didn't bode well for Laura and Chase's short time with us. I was seized with consternation that their whole trip would be through uninspiring terrain and that they would hate it. Luckily, Wenk was only referring to a short stretch between Deer Creek and Duck Creek and, even so, we enjoyed everything about the trail, even that part. We all found the first burned-out section after Red's to be very interesting, the scorched tree trunks standing erect like black sentinels. We camped near Red Cones, two noteworthy symmetrical reddish cinder cones that may have erupted 8,500 years ago. Beyond that, the healthy forested sections of lodgepole and western white pines were full of gaps, allowing magnificent views of the Silver Divide's canyon walls plunging down to Fish Creek, where we were headed. Even the flat trail of pumice sand and granitic gravel was varied and pleasant, reminding us of the tremendous forces of nature that ground the stone to grit. None of us found any of it boring, though admittedly it wasn't quite as striking as other parts of the Sierra.

Laura and I had so many things to talk about, comparing notes on all of our summer adventures, that we completely lost focus on the trail. We chatted with everyone who came along, including Maui Russell from the JMT Yahoo Group and DC Boy (Lucas), an eighteen-year-old solo hiker from Washington DC. Chase finally said, "That's it, I'm hiking between you two so we can keep moving." That was the end of girl talk, but Chase's chatter was just as enjoyable. What fifteen-year-old still likes to hang around with parents and godparents? I loved having him along, even if he did make us wait to zip on his extra-ventilated, partially zipped-off pants before every photo so he didn't look goofy—for the girls back home, I presumed.

I thought back to when I met Laura, nearly 20 years ago, when our ski buddy, Ken introduced us to a "new girl." Having known some of his old girlfriends, we were a bit skeptical. Would she be too girly, not able to keep up on the slopes and spend time primping at the mirror? No, on all counts! If anything she was the most competent skier among us and refreshingly down to earth. We were so honored when they asked us to be godparents to Chase a few years later. A little thing like pregnancy didn't slow her down and she still skied the steeps at Squaw Valley with her eight months pregnant belly sticking out, filling out Ken's ski suit nicely.

A few years later I considered what I could offer Chase and his big sister, Taira, that they didn't already have. They had plenty of toys, attended every kind of enrichment activity and camp anyone could think of, skied on the Mighty Mite team and led a generally wonderful life. I hit on the idea of backpacking since that was a skill their parents lacked. I believed that the gift of spending time with them while teaching valuable skills and exposing them to nature was about as good as it gets. Taira, like her mom, took the trails with gusto, never complaining, offering to take more weight and hiking steadily. Chase, on the other hand, liked his creature comforts, rejected the small daypack outright and sulked when the wind blew too hard. But he was only four years old, so he could be forgiven. By the time he was six and graduated to a real pack with structure and a waist belt, he was good for a few miles as long as there was some water to play in at the end. Every summer we planned a backpacking trip in Tahoe, gradually increasing the length and difficulty until Taira and Ken cried uncle, declining to do any more backpacking. Taira's excuse was water polo (but it could have also been that affliction known as teen years) and Ken's excuse was Taira (someone had to stay home with her). Chase kept on going, though. It was wonderful to be able to plan longer trips and it wouldn't be long before he would be leaving us in the dust. It had already happened on skis, and he delighted in looking bored at the bottom of the hill, waiting for us to come down an expert slope.

The person who got the most inspired by backpacking was Laura. She took to it like a duck to water, accumulating all the gear, leading Boy Scout troops on backpacking trips and joining active backpacking forums. She was determined not to let her knee interfere with the 50-mile loop she had planned for this rendezvous with us and worked hard in physical therapy to be ready. We were dubious, but should have known better. This was Laura, after all. And here they were, ready to hit the trail.

Chase and Laura did so many thoughtful things for us to ease the burden of the second, longer section.

"We'll take your garbage out for you."
"Chase, pump some extra water for them so they can save their batteries."
"Here, take some extra brown sugar."

They cheerfully wedged into an overcrowded spot teeming with backpackers at Duck Pass Junction, and nattered with our many nearby neighbors. Chase was sweet when I encouraged him to hike ahead with Steve the next day. He said, "Make sure my mom is okay. Stay with her." He was worried that her recently repaired knee wouldn't hold up. Chase's rapidly growing feet threatened to poke through his boots, making for sore paws, so we made sure to stop every few hours to give them a rest. He changed his socks and soaked his aching bipeds whenever we found water.

As for the trail, first there was the dramatic amphitheater of chilly Purple Lake, where we were surrounded by the likeness of a multicolored sand pit from the slough-off of metamorphic and granite rock. Then there was Virginia Lake, with its warmer water and wide-open, welcoming shoreline. Besides the lakes we found more than a few creeks along the way that were perfect foot-dipping spots. We sat by streams and listened to water rippling over rocks and logs, swirling into deeper pools where multicolored gravel settled on the bottom to gently massage our grimy feet.

Steve kept getting ahead while Laura, Chase and I dawdled, taking photographs of every bird, flower and vista until, toiling down Tully Hole, he called up to us. "I'd get a move on if I were you—I don't like the looks of those clouds." He pointed to an ominous-looking dark cloud bank that had settled on the ridge top.

"Yikes," I said to Laura and Chase. "We'd better kick it into high gear." Cameras were stowed, and I lent one of my hiking poles to Laura so she could hobble a little more effectively down the steep, exposed switchbacks. "We don't want to be caught here if lightning strikes."

We scurried as fast as we could, catching up to Steve at Fish Creek. There, we all stood gawking at the large brook trout flashing their vivid colors in the stream. Tall lodgepole pines rose from the constricted canyon, barely wide enough for the creek and a narrow footpath, with rock walls rising and widening into a "V" shape at the top of the canyon where we had been walking hours before. A steady sprinkle gradually became more insistent, transforming into thick droplets of water that plopped onto the trail, bouncing off the fine, dry dust.

We dashed across a sturdy metal bridge spanning a deep chasm of foaming water and began searching for tent sites in a clearing. To our dismay, the geometric lines of solo tents were found behind every boulder. This neighborhood was already occupied. Scrambling over large rocks, we dropped down to a slightly angled ramp next to the river.

"Better check to see what would happen if the river became engorged," I said.

Steve peered through the foliage, reporting that there was plenty of room for the river to rise. But that neighborhood was also occupied, this time by large ant colonies that streamed out from under every stone and log we dislodged. Shifting further downstream, we found two acceptable sites, throwing our tents up just in the nick of time.

The whooshing sound of the wind whipping through the tops of the trees was interrupted by a large craaaack of thunder. Brilliant flashes of lightning shone through the tent. My eyes were riveted in the direction of the radiant bursts of light. I counted one-one-thousand, two-one-thousand, up to ten-one-thousand, a comfortable gap. They got closer and closer. They were five seconds apart, then, "Oh, my, that's right outside," I said to Steve. An ear-splitting crack followed the flash instantly. I sat up, drawing my knees to my chest, trying to round my shoulders so that

I wasn't touching either of the metal hoops that held our tent up. Flash. Craaaaack. Flash. Crack. I stretched out, laying down flat, thinking that would help relax me. Steve said, "You're better off sitting. Make yourself a small target, not a long one." Up I shot, fidgeting with my glasses, camera, phone, ear buds...anything to try to take my mind off of my impending death by lightning. I tried to read but the words jumped off the screen with every jolt. I put my earbuds in and squeezed my eyes shut but I could still see the flash of light through my eyelids. My eyes flew open as I strained to look through the tent with X-ray vision. I made peace with death, sorry that Chase was going to have childhood trauma from seeing my dead, scorched body. Hopefully Laura would send him to a therapist. *Oh, no, maybe Chase was scared, too*, I thought. He had never been one for loud noises, covering his ears during fireworks and wailing during windy snow storms when he was a toddler.

"Chase," I called out to the other tent. "Are you all right?"

"Doing fine," came the nonchalant reply. "That was a close one."

"What are you doing?" I asked.

"Playing cards with mom," he said. He sounded pretty calm and if he was playing cards maybe he wasn't quaking as much as I was. He probably wasn't speculating that the narrow canyon was funneling the lightning right down to our two little tents. "Owww," said Chase.

"What's wrong?" I asked, terrified that lightning had struck.

"Hail on my head," said Chase, just as a large chunk of ice found its mark on my own head, right through the thin fabric of the tent.

"Ow is right," I said. Steve laughed until his head became a target.

"Wow, you're not kidding," Steve said, rubbing his skull.

I didn't check in with Laura. I didn't need to. Nothing ever fazed her.

The hail really started coming down in earnest. I distracted myself from the cracks of thunder, though I still jumped with each flash of lightning, by taking videos of the hailstones bouncing off the ground like little jumping beans. Soon, but not soon enough for me, the storm moved down the canyon, leaving us with an exceedingly soggy campsite. I fretted that this wasn't the sort of trip Chase and Laura had dreamed of, especially when Chase dragged out some soaked clothing and a wet shoe that had been positioned perfectly to collect the wrath of the storm. But he seemed to take it in stride. Where did all this new-found maturity come from? My anxiety from the lightning storm and worry that Chase wasn't having a good time drained away slowly as we got our dinner supplies out. Laura emerged from her tent with a smile and showed us the pictures she took of the hail, happy as a clam.

I was taken aback as I watched Steve gather tiny twigs around the campsite. We had vowed to not have any campfires during this drought-infested summer, but there he was building a little pyramid and lighting a match. Were we in the narrow elevation band where fires were allowed? What park were we in? We had been given a sheaf of papers when we got our permit that outlined fire and camping regulations in several of the parks we went through but I wasn't sure where we were. I considered getting out the maps and cross referencing with the stack of regulations but I was exhausted from the anxiety of the storm and fatigue from hiking so I gave up. The ground was soaked with rain so the fire danger was low and I was cold.

"Chase, you little pyro, want to help Steve gather sticks?" I asked, knowing that he loved fire.

"Oh yeah, that sounds good." Off he went, happily foraging for slender dry branches hidden under protective, umbrella-like foliage. Presently, the most cheerful bantam-sized fire was crackling, spreading an optimistic glow through the gloom. That simple flame warmed our chilled limbs and chased away the damp melancholy that had threatened to invade our camp. After our dinner of hearty beef stroganoff, we shared some chocolate and tequila (for the adults only) around the campfire, which further warmed us. Later we formed a conga line down to the raging river, scooping up buckets of water with our bear barrels. We laughed while slipping on the moist duff and slick rocks, passing the water from one person to the next to quench the fire.

Steve saved the day with the fire, the only one of the trip, and I was glad to have Chase and Laura's companionship. We packed in a lot of good times for having spent only three nights together. I knew I would miss the two of them. I realized that I had barely thought about mileage or Ralph's progress the last three days as I reveled in their company. The easy days were over and we'd have to start making our miles again once our pals were gone.

Chapter 5: Silver Pass

The next morning we split off toward our first pass of this section, waving goodbye to Chase and Laura as they continued down Fish Creek to do a loop back to Red's. I was a little misty-eyed. *I'll come back and do it with Laura, and hopefully, Chase, when her knee is better,* I vowed to myself. I turned toward the pass, feeling strong.

Silver Pass (10,740 feet, 3274 m) was our first really tough pass, starting with a moderate ascent that wound around pretty Squaw Lake fringed with trees, and ending with an intense incline up the solid granite headwall behind Silver Pass Lake. It wasn't on anyone's list of hardest passes but after the rest day at Red's and three easy days with Chase and Laura it was hard to get back in the flow. Rising steadily in elevation, the air thinned and I couldn't get a deep breath on the switchbacks. Watching Steve lean on his poles, hanging his head down to catch his breath, I thought, *what are we doing here?* Five months after a heart attack, no matter how mild, maybe wasn't the smartest thing to be doing, even if he did have his cardiologist's approval.

We had just returned from a week of hard skiing at Whistler with our Vancouver friends, all expert skiers. Steve had been uncharacteristically fatigued all week, coming in early, backing off of challenging runs he would normally be amped up to do and going to bed early. Nevertheless, he accompanied our friend Tony on Khyber Pass, an out-of-bounds route that stretched two miles through heavily forested, steep terrain.

He chalked his lethargy up to age saying, "I guess I was bound to slow down at some point." He was annoyed, though, staring down the barrel of his 65th birthday. It was coming up in a month and selecting Medicare plans and being bombarded with AARP solicitations was an unpleasant reminder of advancing age.

Two days later we were back at home in California, taking care of all the household and backyard chores that pile up in a week. I saw Steve sitting on our garden bench, not a usual pose for a man who is perpetually in motion. He was lightly rubbing his chest. "What's wrong? Did you hurt yourself?" I asked, used to a litany of minor injuries related to welder sparks, ladders collapsing in fruit trees and ricocheting tools.

"I don't know. I feel funny," he said.

"Funny how?" I asked.

"I don't know. Kind of woozy," he said.

Nurses, who can usually be counted on to be sympathetic in the workplace, aren't known to mollycoddle family members or themselves. Ever practical, I said, "You're probably just dehydrated. Go inside and drink some water. You know how you are. You get out there doing yard work in the heat of the day and you don't drink enough water. I'm going into Santa Rosa to do some errands. I'll be back in awhile." But I didn't leave. Something made me stay. I fiddled around on my computer for a half an hour, then got my purse and found him in the living room, still rubbing his chest. "Ok, I'm taking off. Do you feel better?"

"Not really," he said.

"Why are you rubbing your chest? Do you have indigestion?" I asked.

"Something feels funny," he said once again.

"What does funny mean?" getting exasperated with the "funny" word. "Do you have chest pain?"

"No, not pain exactly," he said.

"Do you have pain in either of your arms?" I asked, running down the list of heart attack symptoms without any real concern.

"No," he said. We went around in circles for a while with this line of talk, getting nowhere. Communication deteriorated further.

"Do you need to go to the doctor?" I asked.

"I don't know, you're the nurse," he said.

"I don't know, I'm not feeling the symptoms," I said. "Is what you're feeling bad enough to go to the ER?"

"How would I know that?" he asked.

"Well, I can't diagnose you without diagnostic equipment," I said, avoiding our usual banter that all I knew was oncology, everything else was unfamiliar ground and that I hadn't been at the bedside in ages. Finally I considered what I did have, the old-fashioned physical assessment tools I had been taught in nursing school. I was certain that would tell me absolutely nothing. I took his pulse. It was wildly irregular and I could barely count the beats per minute. Hmmm. Maybe something was actually going on. I got my old stethoscope out of the back of the medicine closet. Nope, his heart rate was still erratic. What else could I do? Wait, didn't I have a blood pressure machine? I dug out it out of the bottom of the linen closet and hoped the batteries were still good since I hadn't used it in years. I took his blood pressure, fully expecting it to be normal. Wrong. It was sky high.

By the time we got to the hospital, Steve felt fine, but blood tests confirmed that the man least likely to have heart problems had had a heart attack and twelve hours later a clot was removed from an artery and he had a stent. If it had happened two days earlier, on Khyber Pass, it could have been ugly. His appraisal was typically Steve: "It was a small problem, it was fixed and now I'm good for another 20,000 miles." My response was delayed. Then it started to sink in and I struggled to rearrange a new world order where Steve was vulnerable. I was scared, sad, disoriented and numb. I hiked a lot to try to clear my head and eventually found my footing again. His 65th birthday a few weeks later was poignant and boisterous at the same time as our many friends helped him celebrate his new lease on life.

Our plans for the JMT were put on hold. But a few months later, after a stress test, his cardiologist proclaimed him good to go. "I don't have many patients that look like you," he said approvingly. Five months after the heart attack, we were on the John Muir Trail.

I was worried now, though. It was one thing to talk in the abstract about following your dreams, but it was quite another to be in the remote wilderness with an uncertain heart. We'd never considered having a communication device in the wild, where cell service was spotty at best, but I was glad I had the SPOT satellite messenger safely strapped to my pack. With the push of a button, I could summon help from the nearest Search and Rescue (SAR) organization and our GPS coordinates would be transmitted via satellite. If needed, however, it would still take an uncomfortably long time to get help. So I pushed myself to catch up, saying, "Let's just take a mini-break here and let our heart rates settle down."

"I'm fine," he said.

"I know you are, but my heart rate is up there, too. So let's just stop here together for a minute," I said. We stood at a bend in the switchback, breathing heavily.

"I don't want to cramp up," said Steve, more worried about lactic acid in his legs than his stent blowing up.

"Okay, let's go to the next switchback and pause," I said.

I paced us going up the last steep kick, stopping after each bend of the switchback to take several slow breaths. I was worried that Steve wouldn't want to play my game, but he stopped with me each time and we each caught our breath, only to walk a few paces and lose it again.

We made it to the top and plunked down silently near some taciturn people. No one was chattering or telling stories, so we just ate our lunch quietly. When I asked one of the guys to take our photo he seemed reluctant, but acquiesced. There was no evidence of a trail community in this place, but I didn't care. I was just glad we made it safely and looked forward to the descent when I wouldn't be wracked with worry about Steve.

We stopped at a gurgling stream in a wooded area underneath rocky spires a few miles later to fill up our water bottles, using our SteriPEN to purify the water with ultraviolet light. While answering nature's call, I came upon the most amazing mushrooms, some larger than my foot. Several were symmetrically round, others crazily misshapen, and the death cap (Amanita muscaria) wore a garish red hat with white polka dots. I couldn't tempt Steve to walk an extra few hundred feet. He was content to see them on my camera screen.

Then a strange thing happened as we followed the creek. It looked like we were crossing a low valley, but it turned out to be a very high valley that spread into a large meadow. I could see a large grove of trees at the far edge of the meadow, but then what? I became disoriented, looking down the trail to see if I could pick out the route, only to see it disappear into an airy nothingness. We reached the trees and started descending, but the trail dropped off out of sight. I had a moment of unsettling vertigo as my brain attempted to process mixed signals. Finally, it aligned with the trail traversing left across a huge cliff and descending down a most dramatic gorge. The tumble of peaks layered into the "V" of the valley, but apparently it was so commonplace that the mapmaker didn't even deign to name it. Anywhere else in the world, this majestic scene would be considered a natural wonder, enticing tourists to make the journey to see. However, in the midst of so many other marvels, it didn't garner enough attention to have a moniker. I tried to capture the vista with my camera but could see on the tiny screen that it didn't begin to capture the moment.

On and on we went, across vast slick slabs of polished granite shimmering with sluiced panes of water, through rustling forests, crossing and re-crossing murmuring brooks. Finally we collapsed at Mono Creek, fast moving water tearing across the path, too tired to go on. We picked out a nice spot for our tent among several campsites, flat but protected by tree cover to give us some shelter from the inevitable rain. I was quieter than usual, feeling a bit melancholy after a long day. I was missing the company of Chase and Laura.

After washing up and having tabbouleh and lamb with a faintly Moroccan-flavored marinara sauce, I asked Steve how far we went that day. "Eight point three miles," he replied, after checking his spreadsheet where he was tracking the mileage.

"What? Only eight miles?" I asked. I was discouraged. "I thought we'd be stronger and faster by now, but I still feel like I'm walking my absolute limit every day. Shouldn't we be able to crank out more miles than that, especially with all that downhill?" We were just starting to realize that the downhill portions of the trail didn't equal greater speed. The rough, constantly changing terrain was harder on the knees and hips going downhill.

"That was enough for me for one day, how about you?" Steve asked.

"Absolutely. That's the problem. I don't feel like I can hike more, but I feel like I should be able to go further, or at least not be completely wrung out," I said.

"We're doing well, and we're doing just what we planned to do," he said, trying to reassure me.

As dusk gathered around us, a couple showed up, looking a bit wild-eyed. The slender young woman asked if they could share our campsite while her bedraggled male partner hung back. He looked like he was too tired to talk. "Of course, there's plenty of room here," I said, showing them a large flat site between us and the creek.

"Thank you so much," said the woman, "We're so tired after hiking eighteen miles, and we absolutely have to do twenty miles by 5:30 tomorrow or we'll miss dinner at Muir Trail Ranch."

"No problem," I said. "Twenty miles! Yikes! You're animals." I left them to hurriedly set up camp and get their dinner together in the waning light. It seemed like 20 minutes later they were in their tents with no light showing. They certainly weren't taking any time to relax or read. It would have been nice to talk to them more but, like so many others we had seen so far, our interactions were generic and my impressions one dimensional. Either people were going in the opposite direction and in a hurry, or kept to themselves in couples or small groups, or were too blasted to converse. Actually, that's how I felt a lot of the time. A hike like this wasn't easy, but there was some satisfaction in stripping away social conventions to live life in the moment. When the main concern is protection from the elements, having enough food to fuel one's body and traipsing over challenging terrain it distils life to its pure essence. But I hadn't let go completely.

"Twenty miles," I said, returning to Steve. "Now I feel bad. Why can't I do that?"

"We can't compare ourselves to the youngsters," Steve said. "We're doing fine. We have the time. Hike your own hike, remember?"

I dove in the tent to evade the evening sprinkles and to read through Ralph's account again. "You know that speed record from Ralph that was on the forum?" I called out to Steve. "He did this part in seventeen hours, everything from Island Pass to here."

"You've got to be kidding," Steve said.

"No, I'm not. He hiked 45.6 miles at an average of 2.66 miles per hour, covering everything from our third day to our ninth day in one Ralph-day," I said, incredulous now that I had a better understanding of his feat.

"Let me see that. What was he carrying? What did he eat? How many miles a day did he do?"

All of a sudden we wanted to dissect every detail of Ralph's hike. Luckily I had copied several pieces that Ralph had written at different times, so I had everything there. We pored over each section, including the route, summary, daily journal, kit failures and food list. He had hiked the trail several times at a more leisurely pace, but this was a special effort to see how fast he could do it. "Now I feel REALLY bad. But I guess we're out here doing it, whatever our pace," I said. "There aren't that many people our age out here," I said, consoling myself, then negating it with, "Even though Ralph is fifty." He was just six years younger than I. I put Ralph's account away and resolved to somehow hike stronger.

I wondered how Chase and Laura were faring and wished we were all still together. I didn't think I'd care so much about miles if they were present because it would be more about making sure our little family unit was enjoying the trail. Even though they weren't with us, I liked knowing that they were sleeping outside under the same big sky, only one valley away from us.

Chapter 6: Selden Pass

I wasn't surprised to find the 20-Milers gone already when we arose, having stealthily packed up before dawn. As we passed the junction to Vermillion Valley Ranch (VVR), another resupply spot, I looked longingly at the sign explaining the logistics of the ferry. When we were doing our planning, it had seemed like it would break up this section too much to justify stopping at Red's, VVR and Muir Trail Ranch (MTR). But now, in the thick of it, it seemed like it would have been just about right.

On the next million or so switchbacks, we ran into a group of four, which turned out to be two random couples who happened to have stopped at the same time. One couple in our age range, The Texans, said with a slight twang, "You go on ahead, everyone is faster than we are." Jan, a tiny woman with short brown hair and a bright blue shirt, rested on a boulder with her husband, Jim, a sturdy man, both with Tilley hats like ours.

"I don't know about that, we're pretty slow," I replied, thinking about my discouragement last night. "But these young ones will surely be faster," I said, pointing at the other couple.

The younger man, Gabe, who had a round face and short beard that looked like it had started when he started the trail, said, "No, not us, we're taking our time." His Asian companion nodded in agreement. We shared daily mileage goals and I was surprised to find we were all about the same, aiming for seven to ten miles a day and all planning to be at MTR in two days. I felt good about finding some younger people who weren't necessarily pulling twenty-mile days. We pulled ahead, stopping for a break awhile later. Gabe came along soon after, chatting for a while about medical school, eventually settling in with us as he waited for his partner, Melody, who was also in medical school in Sacramento. We took an extended break and enjoyed socializing with them. We told medical stories, Melody and I sharing a fascination with bustling medical centers that operated like small cities while Gabe strongly preferred rural clinic settings. They both loved the Sierra, but Gabe was hankering to do the PCT while Mel seemed more focused on her budding career. It was obvious she was a driven person, scheduling this trip so tightly that she was expected back at U.C. Davis to teach a seminar to the incoming class of medical students the day after their return. Jim and Jan didn't materialize and we left The Doctors to enjoy their break.

That night at Bear Creek, we saw our one and only bear—a small, skittish yearling that Steve tracked for a fuzzy photo. I scanned the trail often, hoping I'd see one of our new friends from the trail or another bear. We didn't see them that night but talked to a few of our neighbors after we spotted the bear, including Grandma, an elderly Japanese-American woman hiking by herself and The Dog People, a couple with two black labs on a five-day loop in Inyo National Forest, where dogs are allowed. I was interested to see that they kept their dogs inside their three-person tent and was amused at their stories of how the dogs control the pace.

"When she's had enough, she sits in the middle of the trail and won't budge. That's when we know it's time to find a campsite," the man said. Both Grandma and The Dog People, who were practically camped on top of each other, had to cross our campsite every time they fetched water from the stream. We had several brief encounters, not realizing we'd be leapfrogging with each other the next few days.

Grandma was friendly but kept mostly to herself. The first time she approached the creek to fill her water bottles, which she carried awkwardly in her hands, I gestured to several accessible spots. She seemed a bit hesitant as she looked at the thick brush so I showed her the best site, where the foliage opened up to a small gravel beach. I couldn't tell if her English wasn't fluent or she wasn't feeling chatty but after asking her a couple of questions about her solo journey and getting short answers I left her to her water filtering task.

The next morning I eagerly approached Marie Lake, passing through meadows filled with lush green grass, tiny colorful wildflowers and small streams. If it was this pretty down below, how much prettier would Marie Lake be? As usual, the thin air at 10,000 feet sucked all the energy out of me, converting it to lead in my legs, but my mind was clear. The adjustments of the first days on the trail hadn't left much energy for daydreaming, and Laura and Chase had provided much-needed distraction. But now, my mind was wandering unfettered, shapeshifting between the here and now and the otherworld. What would my future hold? A few more years working in the corporate world? More travel? Another long trail? I had hoped that time on the trail would offer up some solutions, but so far all I had were more questions and swirling, unfocused reflections. Although I wasn't even done with this trail, I knew that outside was where I wanted to be.

My love affair with the mountains was not born in childhood. There were no mountaineering ancestors or camping trips in tents, just hardworking Midwestern folk who suffered and thrived in the Dust Bowl. My parents, who had escaped to travel the world, did appreciate nature and exposed me to a multitude of experiences as my father's work as an irrigation engineer took us to far-flung corners of the earth. There were certainly tall mountains in Pakistan and Peru but irrigation work is planned in big, bustling cities and any field work involved dry, dusty deserts far away from water. There is photographic evidence that we visited Kashmir, but I was apparently more interested in catching my first fish and exploring the wonders of a houseboat than noticing mountains. When stateside, we visited the Sierra long enough for me to get on skis briefly but it wasn't a big part of my life.

In my twenties, living the fast-paced life of a San Francisco urbanite, I longed to be outside where green grass and open space could be found. I got away whenever I could and a winter trip to Yosemite with some girlfriends might have been the turning point. The velvety blanket of snow made the park look so clean and wondrous as Half Dome looked over us protectively. Skiing at Badger Pass, where the bell rings in the morning and virtually everyone at the small ski area lines up for ski classes, was special. At the top of the chairlift, I looked at paths leading into the wilderness and wondered what was out there. I wanted to go. When we returned to San Francisco, Eliane and I vowed to return to the mountains as often as we could. We commenced to pull together a group of people from the hospital where we worked to get a ski lease in Tahoe. For years we would do crazy things like work a night shift and drive up to Squaw Valley to ski for a day. I craved the mountains, finding a deep, spiritual peace in the narrow valleys between tall peaks. Clean, white snow resting on the boughs of evergreen fir trees against the blue, blue sky was as good as it got. I found freedom on skis, the graceful, sliding motion making me feel a part of the mountain. As a not-yet-fully-developed adult, I found life lessons in achieving things that I didn't think I could do, from perfecting an effortless carving turn to leaping off small cliffs. I loved becoming airborne and experiencing that moment of free-fall before gently landing on soft, bent knees. I found diminutive spurts of that same free-fall on the steepest flanks just at that precise moment when weight is shifted from one leg to the other and it spurred me on. Summers found me missing my mountains so eventually I started hiking the trails behind the ski area, finding even more to love as I discovered hidden lakes, profuse wildflowers and peaceful solitude. Those were all nice but what really resonated with me were the massive mountains themselves, huge, strong granite cliffs, forest-clad slopes with trees that reached for the sky and dramatic gorges that spoke of tumult. It was the perfect antidote to the clanging, noisy, siren-filled city I lived in. It was a miracle to me that hiking but a few miles could feel so removed from civilization.

Soft footfalls shook me from my reverie. I tried to gauge when to pull over. I didn't like to interrupt my rhythm by turning around all the time, but I didn't want to hold up a faster hiker. Finally I decided it was the right time and pulled off the trail. Glancing up at a tall, friendly-looking, young man, I said, "Hey, I know you, we saw you…." I trailed off trying to place where it was that I had seen DC Boy. At the same time we both said, "Virginia Lake." "That's right. It was with my friend, Laura. How did you get behind us? You have to be so much faster," I said, knowing from our previous encounter that he was only 18, just graduated from high school and heading off to college.

"I stopped at VVR for an extra night," he said, his tousled, caramel colored hair falling over one eye. He had a sweet smile and was a good looking lad.

"Oh, how nice. I wish we had done that. Was it worth it?" I asked.

"It was great. The food was wonderful and the people were nice," he said. Drat, that made me wish even more that we had stayed there. "Do you know what day of the week it is?" he asked.

I tried hard to sort that out but finally said, "I haven't a clue. I couldn't even hazard a guess." What a marvelous feeling—I didn't know what day it was and had no need to know.

"I think it's Sunday—do you know if MTR is closed, or if they close early on Sunday?" He looked worried.

"I don't know for sure, but I don't remember reading anything about that, so I don't think it matters." DC Boy pulled ahead. "I'll see you at the top," I said, but I never did see him again that day.

I found Steve, who had pulled ahead as usual, at the shore of Marie Lake. It was as nice as I had heard, but very exposed. We had had several days of thunderstorms behind us so I immediately said, "Very pretty, but I'm not staying here with all this lightning." The backdrop of dramatic, pyramidal peaks behind the lake dotted with long, granite islands and jutting peninsulas gave the impression of many lakelets and channels, though it was all one. A few dwarf trees populated the islands, but it was otherwise rocky with low bushes, and wouldn't give much protection from the impending storm.

We found some flat rocks to sit on against a large boulder and stopped for a hasty lunch of corn soup thickened with instant potatoes that filled our burrito. It was cut short when I noticed what was going on just behind Selden Pass (10,900 feet, 3,322 m), only 350 feet higher.

"Oh shoot. Look at that—she's early today," referring to the daily storms we had been getting.

Dark clouds were gathering in the not so far distance. As I was tearing my string cheese into thin threads a few minutes later, The Doctors passed by and, after exchanging warm greetings, they said they were going to try to beat the storm. After they departed I asked Steve, "Do you think we should wait, or get over now?" After debating for a split second, we decided to make run for it, tossing the remains of our lunch in my pack and scampering as fast as we could toward the pass.

As we started up the last pitch, I could see The Doctors about four switchbacks ahead of us. I still had to take rest breaks at each directional change, but I tried to make them last only a few seconds instead of my usual five or six deep breaths, my heart fluttering in my chest like a wounded bird. I hoped Steve's heart was okay. The choice presented to me wasn't an easy one. Did we stop and get hit by lightning? Or did we keep going only to have me stress about his heart? Neither was appealing. I reviewed the ABCs of CPR in my head: check airway, breathing then circulation.

Just as we went over the broad, somewhat anticlimactic pass, a peal of thunder rumbled. We didn't even pause for the obligatory photo. Charging down the rough trail, we planted our trekking poles together to swing our legs hastily over the uneven terrain, giggling nervously and making morbid jokes as we set a personal best for our fastest descent ever. When Steve said, "You know, you never showed me how to use the SPOT," I knew he was thinking the worst, as I had. The SPOT satellite messenger device that I carried had an SOS button that would summon the nearest search and rescue personnel to our GPS location.

"If we make it down alive I'll show you tonight," I said. "Let's try to stay with The Doctors. What year of medical school are they in? Surely they've been taught CPR by now. Two-man CPR is so much easier than solo." We covered the next two miles in a flash, flying on the wings of adrenaline.

We caught up to The Doctors as they paused to put their pack covers on. The hail started pelting down on us and I threw over my shoulder, "Just let me know when you want to pass." They followed close behind and the four of us raced down the mountain at record speed, zooming by Heart Lake with barely a glance as hail stones bounced off our heads. "Another pretty lake, but still too exposed," I called out breathlessly. "Not worth stopping."

We pulled up at tranquil Sallie Keyes Lake, which looked like a different, much calmer planet in another universe. "Let's stay here," I said to our little band of survivors, but The Doctors didn't trust the weather and continued on. "See you at MTR," I said as we waved good bye, and then tried to settle down. I felt like I could have walked ten more miles. It would have been nice to hang out with The Doctors, but I honored Steve's request to camp by a lake and this was the last lake for a while. We had discovered that I prefer the clear running water of creeks, even though they are colder, while he favored calm lake waters, even though the bottoms were squishy with mud. We tried to mix it up when picking camp sites.

Every hiker on the trail had talked about the weather and how unusual it was, but that night, perusing the Wenk book, I found a section on weather. She described the "monsoon moisture" we had been experiencing perfectly. It often originates from a tropical storm to the south, resulting in the slow buildup of cumulus clouds that arrives a bit earlier each afternoon and looks more menacing. So there we had it. All that "unusual" weather we had been experiencing was perfectly normal, though not necessarily an every-year occurrence.

We enjoyed Sallie Keyes Lake a lot. The reflection of the pointed tips of green trees and soft outlines of layers of plump clouds were painted onto the mirror-silver lake. The serene still-life invited quiet contemplation. Every once in awhile the gentlest of breezes created fine ripples that lapped against the shore to remind us who was in charge and we gave thanks to Mother Nature for this respite. Rolling hills behind our tent were so different from the rugged terrain we had been on for days that it even tempted me to explore our surroundings. Most evenings I was so tired that I barely moved from the campsite but here I strolled easily among the giant trees and found many empty campsites on the wide peninsula that bisected the lake. It had been a good day and this was a happy place.

I thought about the 20-Milers and envisioned them sitting down to a great big barbecue with chicken, ribs, potato salad, green salad, coleslaw, beer and ice cream. I had no idea what MTR served for dinner, but it didn't matter since I wasn't getting any. Our corn, bean and squash stew would have to do.

Chapter 7: Muir Trail Ranch

I was so excited to get to MTR that I woke early to impatiently eat breakfast, break down camp and fly down the mountain as fast as my legs would carry me. As we traversed the hillside, we could see a strip of brown at the bottom of a deep valley by a clearing that looked man-made. I knew it had to be MTR, and that put wings on my feet. Soon we were descending a series of switchbacks in heavily forested terrain. As we got closer we could see a large horse corral, a few small sheds and a series of rustic log cabins all set around a broad meadow. As soon as we went through the gate we were immediately reunited with The Doctors, The Texans and DC Boy. After a round of hugs like long lost friends, we all gaped together at the huge assortment of hiker barrels lined up against the corral fence, each labeled with its contents. This collection of free stuff consisted of discards from overly ambitious hikers who had sent the kitchen sink in their resupply buckets. Packaged meals, homemade meals, snacks, drinks, toiletries, maps, clothing and more were barely contained in at least 20 five-gallon buckets, most filled to the brim. It was completely overwhelming. "Look at this humongous jar of Nutella," Steve exclaimed. "It must weigh five pounds."

We retrieved our two buckets after presenting our claim check, having splurged by sending a second bucket so we could eat well during our zero day. Almost one whole bucket was just for food we planned to eat at MTR while the other would have to fuel us for the next ten days. Some hikers weren't staying so they retrieved their resupply bucket from the storage shed, opened the top and stuffed as much as they could in their packs. The rest they tossed into the hiker barrels for others to sort through at will. After we laid out our food under a large canopy, I was even more overcome. I spent most of the time chatting with other hikers while mindlessly arranging everything in like-groups—all the energy bars here, all the lunches there—without actually making any sense of it. Finally Steve came over and rescued me by stuffing all the food in our canisters, but not until we made a few exchanges with some of the hiker barrels. I was already sick of some our soups and was happy to drop them off in exchange for some tuna packets—real food! I wondered why we sent anything at all since it was obvious that if you weren't picky there was plenty of free food to resupply for the next ten days. Steve picked up some fuel to use while we were at MTR and some extra batteries. The battery bucket was full of AA and AAA batteries.

We even ran into the 20-Milers, who did make it in time for dinner the night before, sort of. The girl made it, but the guy was dragging so much that she ran ahead and saved him a plate. It turned out he was having some kind of gastro-intestinal problem and they were bailing. Argh. All those twenty-mile days and where did it get them? Not to the end, that's for sure. It was no fault of theirs, but it reinforced that there was nothing wrong with our slow and steady pace, like the fable of the tortoise and the hare. I offered the guy some sympathy and Pepto-Bismol tablets to ease his uncomfortable hike out.

I walked over to the tiny store, a shed made from rough-hewn shakes with a blue tarp-covered tin roof, hoping they'd have some snacks for purchase. I knew the remote camp in this roadless area only had the capacity to feed their paying guests staying at the cabins, not the hordes of thru-hikers coming through. But I hoped I'd be able to get some kind of treat, like chips or cookies—no such luck. They only sold a few sundries, such as batteries and insect repellent, at the store.

The historic ranch, in private hands since 1885 and owned by the current family since 1953, was first used by cattlemen and shepherds driving their herds to the high country meadows. Before that, Native Americans, who camped at what is now called Blayney Meadow, came over Piute Pass to trade with other tribes in the foothills. The people at MTR now cheerfully endure the tedious tasks required to pick up, transport, deliver, log and store resupply buckets in this isolated location. They had to handle each bucket at least twelve times. So I didn't mind too much that they didn't have a bag of chips or a cold beer. Well, maybe I did mind the cold beer part.

We had decided to forego the expensive cabins, wanting to stick with the pure hiker experience of tenting the whole trip. I didn't regret our decision to sleep in our tent, but I would have paid an embarrassingly large sum for a hot shower. The Texans came over and said, "Hey, our room is really cute. Feel free to come over and use the bathroom any time you want,"

"Oh wow," I said, my hopes soaring. "A shower?"

"No such luck. Showers are in the central bathhouse fed by hot springs. Only paying guests are allowed in there," said Jan. We went over anyway to check out the cabin. The sturdy log structure had a double and twin bed with matching colorful covers and pillows, but no sheets as guests are expected to use their sleeping bags. It was fun to flush the toilet, but I sorely missed that shower. I did enjoy splashing some cool water on my face from the sink faucet.

Finally, we stuffed our packs back together and took one heavy plastic bucket, toting it between us on the rough trail. The designated camping area was tucked well away from the paying guests. The Doctors had already set up and came over to show us the best spots. We picked one, then directed DC Boy to one near us when he arrived. Later, Grandma and The Dog People showed up and we all circulated around to each other's tents, chattering about the trail and examining equipment. The Doctors already had their laundry hanging on the line, having washed it near the river. I looked around at our little community with a sense of satisfaction—the trail life I had read about in so many other people's narratives was coming alive for us.

The ranch wasn't the only place to experience hot springs. We knew Blaney Hot Springs were available for all to enjoy and were directed across the river by a few people we asked. After surveying the swift flow of water, I gripped my hiking pole and carefully stepped in, fervently hoping my flip flops would stay on. At first it wasn't bad. But as I approached the deeper channel, the tug of water became more profound and the roar of the river filled my ears. I stepped carefully so as not to stumble on the slippery rocks, making certain that my pole was planted securely before lifting a foot. I wondered if the infamous Evolution Creek crossing in a couple of days would be worse. I slowly made my way across, finally stepping out of the cold water onto a well-worn path with relief. A young woman who had forgotten her hiking pole shouted that she was too afraid to cross and she'd see us later.

We looked at the multitude of social trails going in all directions, picking one going to the right. We found ourselves in a meadow with tall grass and no hot springs in sight. I don't know what we were expecting, maybe a sign with "Blaney Hot Springs" or a hot dog stand manned by Mr. Blaney, or perhaps a concrete tub like at Kern Hot Springs on the High Sierra Trail. We continued walking and were startled to find the round faces of The Doctors sticking out of the ground like bobble-heads. They waved us over. "Come on in, there's plenty of room," said Mel, gesturing at the muddy water they were sitting in. "There are some other holes, but this one had the cleanest water," she said, adding, "Well, before we got in and stirred everything up," after she noticed me doubtfully staring into chocolate-colored water.

"Okay, maybe we'll come back after we check out the other springs," I said. We continued down the path, finding another murky pond a little way away. "Look," I said, "It has a log across it. I wonder if that's to hang on to." Steve went to check for other ponds while I gingerly lowered myself into the muck wearing my hiking shorts and a black sports bra that doubled as a bathing suit top. Finding squishy mud at the bottom that threatened to eat my flip flops I felt around with my feet until I hit solid ground. Someone had kindly placed large flat rocks below the suspended log. Perfect. I stood on the rocks, balancing myself by hanging onto the log and let the warm healing water do its magic on my aching muscles.

Steve came back and joined me, not finding anything better, exhaling a long "Ahhhhhhh," as he lowered himself in. Improbably, strains of jazz music from a clarinet floated through the air like wisps of a forgotten time. Where was that coming from? Mr. Blaney's ghost? We couldn't tell, but it was such a perfect accompaniment that we gave ourselves over to enjoying the treat. It felt every bit as special as paying for mud baths at a fancy spa, complete with live music.

While we were soaking, another hiker came over, still loaded down with his pack. "That creek crossing was the worst of anything I've been on, way worse than Evolution."

"Are you going NOBO?" I asked.

"Yes, and I crossed Evolution today—piece of cake."

"Oh good," I said. "That's one less thing for me to worry about. Come on in." He found a campsite not far away, dumped his pack and slid into a smaller individual sized pond near us. With our heads just barely visible we talked back and forth through the tall grass that veiled the hidden pools. I peppered him with questions since he was walking northbound and had just covered the terrain we would be hiking.

After thoroughly stirring up all the muck we checked out the larger pool, meeting two teens doing the trail by themselves. One of the boys had done the trail at thirteen with his dad and now, at sixteen, was accompanying his fifteen-year-old buddy. Both home-schooled in Sonora, the trip was forming many parts of their school projects, from the planning to the history of the trail to leadership and self-sufficiency—what better way to get educated? They were remarkably self-composed, confident and happy, fishing their way through every hole they could find on the trail.

After walking back to join The Doctors, who now had DC Boy submerged with them, we soaked some more, loath to leave the warm embrace of the mud. The conversation was congenial, roving between hearing about DC Boy's small Quaker college that he would be attending in a few weeks, Mel's hope to be able to stay in Davis for her internship next year, and vignettes from the trail. All of us were concerned about the next section, which we knew would challenge us even more than we had been already. We debated which passes would be the worst and if everyone had enough time to finish based on their schedules and enough food to sustain us. All rhetorical questions since no one would have answers until we got to the end.

"Did you hear that music? I followed the trail behind those bushes and it looked like a bunch of hippies," DC Boy said with wide eyes. "I couldn't tell if they had bathing suits on so I turned around and left quickly." We laughed at his innocence, but still enjoyed the music.

When we had turned to chocolate-covered prunes we all headed back, Steve leading the way. He went this way and that, trying to find the social trail we came in on, his dripping flock dutifully following—that is, until he plunged into a concealed hole just big enough for his right leg, all the way up to his hip. We all collapsed into fits of laughter as he pulled his leg out, crying "My shoe, it has my shoe," quickly thrusting his whole arm in. He withdrew the prize, one very muddy shoe, his arm dripping brown sludge. He grinned while we tried to compose ourselves, finally finding the river where Steve had some serious cleaning to do.

We forded the river back to the campsite to find a sea of shiny Spandex. It was Lululemon gone wild as a group of about twenty people on a yoga backpacking trip filled in every conceivable flat space among our little group. They provided hours of entertainment as we watched women helping each other set up tents that they clearly hadn't looked at in years, most of them bulky car-camping tents that required a lot of fussing. Steve said, "I bet I could sell a lot of the Sierra Designs tents like the one we have if I could do a one-minute demo for them." A lot of stretching and Downward Facing Dog transpired after their camps were set up.

I washed up in the river and changed into my evening clothes, which included my pants and a long-sleeved shirt. My little square of a camp towel was exceeding its capacity for drying, but the low humidity of the Sierra air took care of that. Steve was content to read in his folding chair so I wandered back to the ranch to see what was happening. Jan called me over to their cabin and said, "Want some whiskey? Our neighbors are bringing some over."

Whiskey, yuck. "Sure, I'd love some," I said, always up for a social event. Beggars can't be choosers out here in the wild. It's not like there was a liquor store with a bottle of chilled chardonnay or bar with draft beer around here. Jan brought out an array of plastic cups from the bathroom that crinkled if squeezed too tightly. Two women in their thirties from the cabin next door presented a large glass bottle of whiskey about half full. They looked very clean and put-together.

"Did you send that in your resupply?" I asked incredulously. These two refined ladies didn't look like the type, whatever a whiskey drinker looks like.

"No, the guys leaving our cabin passed it on to us. It's a little bit of trail magic," one said as she poured a little in my cup.

"Not too much," I said, knowing it wasn't really my thing. I took a sip. Mmmm, that wasn't too bad. Lovely warmth seeped into my ravaged muscles.

"Would you like some more?" the bottle-bearing woman asked a little while later.

"Sure, why not?" I said, holding my cup out like I guzzled whiskey all the time.

Thus passed a most enjoyable hour of lively conversation about the JMT, other trails and adventures around the world as the whiskey flowed. Jan and Jim were passionate about water rights since they owned a ranch in drought-stricken Texas, I shared some behind-the-scenes stories about volunteering at a California state park and the two gals with the whiskey talked about their travels as flight attendants. When the conversation veered to other topics, it soon became evident that my liberal philosophical and political leanings were completely opposite of the young ladies, and suddenly I remembered Steve. He was probably wondering where I was, so I said my goodbyes and wobbled back to our camp, using extra care when stepping over the loose barbed wire separating the haves from the have-nots.

We were pretty excited about our camp dinner, though I'm sure it didn't hold a candle to the barbeque going on at the ranch. We had deliberated long and hard about what packaged food would taste the most like real food and we relished the upcoming menu. We popped open cans of Amy's Organic Chili, emptied them into a big plastic bag and submerged the bag in hot water. When it was sufficiently warm, I added chicken from a foil packet and rehydrated salsa, served it with tortillas and string cheese from our new batch and scarfed it down. It was every bit as good as we anticipated. We fell into a food coma, stretched out on our sleeping mats and drifted off to the gentle sounds of the river riffling over small rocks and the quiet chatter of the Yoga People.

Chapter 8: Zero Day

The Texans and Doctors moved on the next morning, needing to keep to their schedule and DC boy, though he elected to stay another night, was absorbed into an animated group of young people closer to his own age. The Yoga People managed to stuff their car camping gear into their packs and donned colorful, skin-tight togs, ready for a new day of poses, postures and perambulation. A whole new group moved in around us, changing the scene significantly. I missed our group and was almost tempted to pack up and move on, but my quivering muscles reminded me that I really did need a complete recovery day. Plus, I needed to do laundry in the river and, best of all, wash my hair.

I had been doing small bits of laundry almost daily, mostly underwear and socks, in an Opsak (a thick zip-top bag). But for a real load of laundry, I used an eight-liter waterproof stuff sack, cramming all of our well-worn clothes into the bag. I hauled it down to the river, filled it with water and added a few drops of bleach. After mashing it around for a few minutes I carried it back to the camping area to discard the dirty water away from the river, then returned to the river for the rinse cycle. I pulled my black sports bra out that I had used in the hot springs and wasn't surprised to find layers of brown dirt embedded in the white liner fabric. It took some scrubbing to get that out. I was so happy to know that we'd have a whole set of clean, fresh-smelling clothes for the next couple of days. Steve strung up a long clothesline from the length of rope he carried for emergencies. We slid the rope through arm or leg holes, tied socks on to secure them and draped towels over the rope, leaving the dripping clothes to dry in the weak sun.

Next on the agenda was the shampoo. It was cool out, so I didn't relish the idea of immersing my head in cold water. Plus, there wasn't enough sun to warm up water naturally. After heating some water in our camp stove, I filled three one-liter water bottles with some boiling water, then added cold water to cool it down. "Steve, can you help me wash my hair?" I asked.

He came over and said, "How are you planning to do this operation?"

I pulled out my small hotel-issue bottles of shampoo and cream rinse that I had packed in our resupply, saying, "Take one Nalgene and slowly pour the water over my head. There's probably enough warm water if you want to wash yours, too."

He replied, "No, I'm fine, but I'll help you," happy to wallow in his hiker sweat. He poured with one hand while he fluffed my short hair with his other, making sure all my hair was wet. I was going to put the shampoo on, but he said, "Give it to me," and lathered up my head, rubbing his fingers into my scalp to give me a head massage like a professional salon. Heaven! He gave me a rinse and we repeated the process with cream rinse, its sweet smelling perfume filling the air.

"Ahhh, I feel like I spent the day at the spa. Are you sure you don't want to wash yours? It feels indescribably delicious." He shrugged in that way that I know means he was thinking about it. I grabbed the last bottle of warm water. "Here, lean over. You won't regret it." We went through the whole process again, even the cream rinse, leaving us both clean as a whistle. Sparkling hair and fresh clothes! What could be better? Who needs that expensive shower over at the ranch?

After my spa experience, I settled down to the task of really sorting through our food—not like yesterday when I had been playing around. Pulling everything out of the barrels, I separated our camp food, which we would consume at MTR, from our hiker food. I put most of the food we'd need later for the next section in my canister, and the rest in Steve's. I tried to take the heavier foods since the food was usually my responsibility and Steve always carried the tent and cooking equipment. I was laying out a lovely display of all of our Clif and Probars when Steve suddenly said, "Oh, no," sitting in his luxury camp chair bent over a tattered and much-revised spreadsheet, pencil smudges covering the entire document.

"What?" I said, groaning to myself. On other trips in the past, this exclamation generally meant that we had miscalculated a critical day. In the Yukon, it meant that we had to paddle extra hours each day until my arms fell off to make up for one day we thought we had but didn't.

"When we took the extra rest day out of the spreadsheet, we deleted the row. But we didn't adjust the dates. We're a day off." Yep, despite endless hours of calculations and spreadsheets, we had done it again. Our table that laid out our daily mileage plan and meals was off by one day.

"Well, at least we're here where we can do something about it, rather than on the trail," I said calmly. "If our end dates are off, we can pay to send an email to the shuttle service and the motel in Mammoth."

"Or, I can rejigger the mileage so we can have some easier days," Steve said,

"Ohhhh, I like the sound of that," I said, mostly because I was dreading the next section, where I knew everything got even harder. "Let's do that."

"But then we'll be short of food," said Steve.

"Again, better that we're here with overflowing hiker barrels than on the trail where we'd have to ration food," I said. "We'll just go through the barrels and hang out under the resupply tent for a few hours and see what comes in."

It had been a lazy day, but now we were on a mission. I quickly sorted through the rest of the food, stashed it in the canisters and headed back to the resupply tent while Steve stayed behind to calculate a new set of daily mileage goals. I plugged my electronics in the power strip that was kindly provided by the proprietors of MTR, and I watched the ebb and flow of hikers who came in, collected their resupply buckets and stared in disbelief at the overflowing hiker barrels. Like a hawk, I watched what they discarded, ambling casually over to snatch a Mountain House meal, some extra oatmeal, tortillas and another tuna packet. Problem solved. Within an hour, we had enough food to fuel us an extra day.

I observed a tall elderly man, slightly stooped as he walked down one of the paths to the cabins. He was accompanied by a woman, presumably his wife, and between them they carried a five-gallon bucket, each holding onto one side of the handle. *What could they be doing*? I wondered. *They couldn't have hiked here, could they*? I knew that visitors could drive to nearby Florence Lake on a rough road and hike five miles to the ranch— maybe they did that? Watching his shuffling steps, I couldn't even imagine him walking five miles, much less with a pack.

Later, when I returned to check on the charging status of my electronics with Steve, I saw the elderly gentleman rummaging through a hiker barrel. "There he is," I whispered to Steve. "That's the guy I was telling you about. Do you think he could be hiking?"

"I don't know. He can barely walk. No way," said Steve after assessing him critically.

I went over and stood next to him.

"What 'cha doin'?" I asked.

"I'm looking for some ramen for my wife. She went through our food and found that we're short one lunch," he said, looking at me briefly. His thin gray hair fell over his thick eyeglasses as he dug through the barrels. White stubble sprouted from his chin.

"Short for what?" I asked, still not believing they could be hiking.

"For the rest of our hike," he replied.

"*What* hike?" I persisted. "The John Muir Trail," he said, looking up at me, staring as if I was a bit slow. "Isn't that what we're all doing here?"

"Yeeeesss," I stuttered, trying to figure out a polite way to ask him how old he was. "I see you have an Appalachian Trail T-shirt on. Have you hiked on that trail?" I asked.

"Oh, yes. My wife and I are trail volunteers in the winter. We ski out six miles to a hut and get it ready for the cross-country skiers. We start the fire, and as people come in we assign sleeping space. I'm seventy-six years old and it keeps me young." There, I had it. Seventy-six years young. I glanced around to see if others were following this conversation, and I saw a bunch of wide eyes. My husband was just shaking his head. Wow, were we all impressed.

"How are you liking the trail?" I asked, wanting to keep the conversation going to find out more about this remarkable man.

"Oh, it's hard, no doubt about it. My wife and our two friends plan an adventure like this every summer. We've hiked all over the Grand Canyon and now we're doing the JMT in sections. We're doing Red's Meadow to Bishop this time. You should meet my buddy. He's eighty-five and going strong."

"Eighty-five!" I exclaimed. "I'd love to meet him. Maybe I'll see him later this afternoon."

"Sure, sure, I'll introduce you. My name is Paul and his is Al."

I made a mental note to write that down before I forgot while he kept picking through packages of food, not finding any ramen. I helped him pick out a few alternate suggestions to see if they passed muster with his wife, and he shuffled off toward the cabins. DC Boy came over and we all excitedly chattered about that amazing interchange and how inspiring it was. I went over to Steve. "And you thought we should do this now because you'd be too old later. Hah, we're just getting started. You've got at least twenty more years to catch up to them." He looked a little nonplussed as we rearranged our preconceived notions in our heads, my hiking horizon suddenly stretching past its previously imagined boundaries.

I told DC Boy that Paul had been looking for ramen, but we couldn't find any. "I know I saw some yesterday. I'll bet it's in the bottom of the barrel," he said, tearing through a bucket. "Here it is," he said, pulling out a package of Top Ramen. He tossed it to me and I ran after Paul.

"Look, we found some ramen. You can add it to the batch and your wife can pick what she wants." He thanked me, looking a bit relieved to have found what she had requested. He slowly turned back toward the cabin, taking his tiny, careful steps through the grass.

A couple of hours later I saw Paul sitting out in the sun with another man. I walked across the meadow and said, "Hi Paul. Is this your hiking buddy?"

"Yes, this is Al." Al was shorter and considerably stockier than Paul, sporting a Buddha belly, thick white beard, bushy white eyebrows and thinning hair on his crown.

"Hi, Al, I'm Inga," I said, shaking his hand. "It's great to meet you. I've been hearing about your exploits from Paul, here. Are you enjoying your zero day?"

"Eh?" he said, peering at me through his eyeglasses, and I realized he was a little hard of hearing.

I repeated my greeting a little louder, to which he said, "I feel great. I'd be on the trail today, but my wife said she had too many chores to do, with laundry and sorting food. So here I sit," Wow, my legs were more than were ready for a day off, and here this octogenarian was raring to go. He looked a lot more robust than Paul, with his thicker body and stronger stride.

When we got back to camp, I relayed the story to The Doctors. They were suitably impressed. Mel said, "You know, Satchyo is eighty-one."

"What? Really? Grandma? The little Asian lady?" It seemed that octogenarians were everywhere, quietly plying the trails, maybe a little slower than others in deference to their age.

"And she's by herself, doing the whole thing, from Yosemite to Whitney," said Mel. I hadn't interacted with Satchyo that much, but my respect for her accomplishments shot up. I resolved to get to know her better. This obsession I had with mileage was silly because I could see that these folks, with their slow but steady steps, could easily out-hike me in a turtle race.

I was glad our miscalculation had prompted me to spend the afternoon meeting these extraordinary hikers and experience more of the camaraderie of the social life of the trail. It boosted my faith that we weren't in over our heads. At least I hoped so, for the last section was lacking in easy outs.

Our second almost-real-food dinner was Sierra Szechwan Chicken Salad, an Asian noodle dish that I had experimented with at home. It had smelled delicious as I made it, but the dish had dehydrated into an incredibly bulky mass of twisted noodles. Although it was lightweight, it would have taken up a quarter of the space of the bear canister. So it had been relegated to a resupply meal. The wide, flat rice noodles, chicken bits and veggies were still delectable, and a packet of soy sauce and Sriracha sauce made it even better.

After dinner, a series of dark thunderclouds moved through, much later than usual. Thunder boomed down the canyon, the sound ricocheting off the walls. But there was only a faint sprinkle of rain, so we barely registered the event.

The new kids on the block were definitely not tired enough, keeping everyone around them awake with recorded music and loud talking long after 10 p.m. I sighed and inserted my ear plugs, hoping I'd feel well rested for the hike out of MTR.

Chapter 9: Evolution

I had been nervous about the next segment for a long time. The passes got bigger, the emergency exits were fewer and those exits that did exist involved additional high passes and rugged, sometimes unmaintained, trails of their own. The first two sections we had done so far felt like training wheels. For crying out loud, Red's was located on a paved road with a big shuttle bus to a real town and Muir Trail Ranch, though more isolated, was only five miles away from a road.

Ralph's written words were imprinted in my brain, "Mather is the most difficult of the big passes," so that was the one I worried about most. But the other ones wouldn't exactly be easy, either. I had also heard that Glen Pass was the worst, and that Muir Pass had an impossibly long ascent, so I considered them all with some degree of trepidation. Muir Pass was the first, so I tried to clear my mind by focusing on one at a time, in order. Hopefully the monsoonal flow was over after six days of daily rains and we were far enough from the raging forest fires to have clear skies free of smoke. I knew we were going to have enough challenges without having environmental factors to contend with.

Our new, more leisurely pace with the extra day in the schedule, along with a glut of heavy food, led to a decision to not pull out of MTR until late morning. We took our time packing up, returning to the hiker tents where I got one more shot of electricity into my phone. This would be the longest stretch so I wanted to start with a full charge for my phone and battery.

The moment of reckoning arrived. It was time to weigh my pack. We had worked hard to reduce our pack weight for the whole trip, but we especially focused on this last section, when we had to carry ten days of supplies on our backs. Over the last couple of years we had discarded our oversized, heavy packs in favor of lighter packs, shaving three pounds off in one fell swoop. Next, we upgraded our tent to one with more headroom and side closets to store our gear and still kept the weight down. We traded our inflatable sleeping pads for one of the new models, discarding not only weight, but a great deal of volume as well. One of my biggest challenges was clothing but I finally adjusted to not carrying changes of clothes. All I had with me for the entire 23 days was one set of hiking clothes, which included a pair of shorts and a pink T-shirt. I wore the same clothes every single day, alternating between two pairs of underwear and two pairs of thin hiking socks. Injinji toe socks and shoes a half size larger than normal had completely eliminated blisters but I liked to alternate the toe socks with a pair of thin, quick drying synthetic socks. I had a separate set of sleeping clothes comprised of hiking pants and a long-sleeved synthetic shirt and thick wool socks. Boy, did I love pulling on those comfortable wool socks every night and putting relatively clean clothes on at night. I knew I could hike in the warmer sleeping clothes if I had to but it never got cold enough. Another item that contributed to good sleep was my small inflatable pillow. Yes, it was a luxury but I couldn't put a price on a good night's sleep. Since we didn't like to hike for endless hours and needed to unwind at night I brought my phone, using apps to read and listen to podcasts. It was well worth the weight for the small device. My camera was important and I chose to carry a tiny, three-ounce solar charger to keep everything juiced up between resupply points. Everything was down to bare bones for us and we were proud of our 25 pound packs with food and water for the first two segments. It wasn't ultralight but our packs were comfortable.

I gingerly placed my pack on the big scale with the meat hook by the resupply station at MTR. The needle danced around as my pack swayed back and forth. Thirty-five pounds, it read. "Not bad," I said, delighted that it wasn't fifty pounds. "That's good because I can't think of a thing I'd leave behind. Let's weigh yours now." Steve hung his pack on the hook. "Forty pounds," I said. He scowled. "Yikes. Well, we'll be eating the food you're carrying first so yours will get lighter before mine," I said.

DC Boy had pulled out early, so we were the last ones of our group to depart. We kept ourselves entertained that last morning watching Benjamin, the four-year-old son of the proprietors, riding a horse. Decked out in his cowboy boots, jeans and ten-gallon hat, he looked like Mini-Me as he climbed up on a big stump near the hitching post. His dad brought a horse over and Benjamin scrambled onto the saddle, taking the reins while following his dad's instructions to get him to turn right or left. After putting him through his paces, he took off with his dad on a trail ride. "We'll be back in a little while," he called out to his mom, as if he took off riding every day. The proud mom came over and told me the horse was thirty-four years old, perfect for a four-year-old, and possessed a gentle and consistent disposition. We all thought that was a pretty cool way to grow up.

Finally we were hungry enough to eat the last of our rehydrated home-made Sierra Szechwan Chicken Salad. Feeling fueled up and rested, we took off.

It was a pleasant, short day, and we bid adieu to the Dog People at Piute Pass in the afternoon. This was one of the possible exit routes and was the last one before entering Kings Canyon National Park, where dogs aren't allowed. We knew that after this we weren't likely to catch up to any of our friends unless they dallied or we speeded up, as everyone was on a schedule.

The climb was gradual. But despite our rest (or maybe because of it), plus the heavier pack, my legs felt like lead. The waters of the San Joaquin River swirled far below us, the deep, green inviting pools vexingly inaccessible from the dusty, rocky trail. Climbing higher, we entered an agreeable lodgepole pine forest with the afternoon sun filtering through the trees next to the burbling creek. For the first time in ages there were no visible thunderheads. Today was supposed to be an easy re-entry day, so we stopped short of a series of switchbacks and found several large welcoming campsites in Goddard Canyon. After setting up camp, I realized that it was probably a pack-animal camp, noting that we had passed a mule train earlier. I don't know what the etiquette is about two people hogging a huge site, but I had a feeling we had made a backcountry faux pas. Luckily no groups came along to kick us out, and we enjoyed lounging around on the "furniture," benches and seats made out of logs. I spent quite a bit of time tracking three does munching on tasty shrubbery near our camp. They took little notice of me as I sat quietly taking their portraits, but they knew I was there. All in all it was a pleasant day, mostly because of our newly found additional day in our schedule. Because of that we were able to walk a few miles and not have to do a big ascent at the end of the day, something that never worked out very well for me.

Dinner was one of our favorites, a kind of Greek meld of orzo, tomato sauce, lamb and turkey mixture, along with lemon oil and freeze-dried grapes that gave it a sweet-tangy yin-yang of flavors. I noticed that a lot of our favorite meals were in our barrels for this stretch, a stroke of brilliant planning since I anticipated some aspects of the trail would be getting old by now.

The next morning we set a new world record for us— getting up at seven, out of camp by eight, and into the freezing cold of the narrow canyon without delay. The price we paid for our location was that there was virtually no warm-up for the steep switchbacks. Up we toiled, one slow-motion step at a time as we gained 750 feet. I was able to hold a fairly consistent pace, being fresh in the morning. We were up out of Goddard Canyon remarkably fast as views of the surrounding peaks came into sharp focus. As always, I scanned the widening horizon for wisps of fluff that could portend rain, but saw nothing but Windex skies. When we neared the top I heard a faint rumbling sound, but I couldn't quite put my finger on it. We traveled higher, the switchbacks angling further to the left. That's when the roar filled my ears. I wanted to see what it was, but the trail curved back the wrong way. So I clambered over some rocks to get closer to the noise. I craned my neck to see if I could see Steve but he was a couple of switchbacks higher.

A wall of water thundered toward me, dropping hundreds of feet into the gorge we had just climbed up, hurling its load into the San Joaquin River far below. Gossamer mist hovered over the drop creating sun-kissed sparkles in the sky. The ethereal film contrasted mightily with the cacophony boiling up from the lathering river. This was the mighty Evolution Creek, the same waterway that struck fear in the hearts of early season hikers with reports of deep water crossings. It was a powerful place to be, and I tried to drink it all in visually.

I didn't tarry, as Steve would be wondering if I fell off the trail. The infamous river crossing, when we got there, turned out to be as uneventful as the guy at the hot springs had said. The river was wide here, narrowing into the slot I

106

had seen, with water barely over my ankles. It was astounding to think that the water could be chest-high in the early season.

Entering Evolution Valley, it was apparent that it was as beautiful as everyone had said. It was an idyllic scene with a meandering creek, lush green meadows and granite spires stabbing at the sky. Horses grazed peacefully like a scene from the Big Valley TV show. It was enough to make me want to throw down my pack and build a log cabin to live out the rest of my days, national park restrictions on that sort of activity notwithstanding. I wanted to stay there forever, but the long valley, with its gentle terrain and endless natural beauty, was over all too quickly. It was apparent from a long way away that there was a towering granite barrier blocking the end of the box canyon, and then we were back to the switchbacks. The conundrum along the whole trail was that when we found the sublime spots, it was almost always easy terrain where we could make our miles. But true to Murphy's Law, the places we ended up camping when we couldn't walk another step were barren slabs of rock with nary a tree.

I had been feeling strong for the first set of switchbacks at the beginning of the day but, after loping along the flat valley for hours, my legs didn't want to hear it when we got to the end of the canyon. They were programmed to do the hard work early and then they were done. Up and up we plodded, reaching for the heavens, the air getting thinner and thinner as we approached 10,000 feet again. My legs screamed for oxygen and I took frequent breaks, implementing a strategy I had used in the past. Take ten steps, then stand motionless and breathe in and out. Repeat. But I was also impatient to see what wonders awaited us at the top, for everything named Evolution was billed as a highlight of the trail. We finally topped out in a rocky area with stunted trees, a few sandy spots and small ponds of water linked by a tiny sinuous stream. It didn't look too promising. However, a bit further on we found the outlet of Evolution Lake, a comely tarn with a few stunted trees.

Campsites were limited as the trail curved around the shore on the only flat terrain, so we camped on a flat finger of sand-covered granite jutting into the water. I lay down on my back to catch my breath and stared for the longest time at the top of this amazing amphitheater. A monstrous wall of light gray granite rose above me, loose scree gathering in pyramidal flows toward the bottom. The serrated ridge sharply contrasted with the cerulean sky. It lost its third dimension, looking unreal, like a flat cardboard cutout against a brilliant blue backdrop. There was something about the convergence of the dramatic scene that made this place transcendent. Maybe it was the hypoxia affecting my brain, but I couldn't get enough of the view. Once my tent was set up, I kept poking my head outside to make sure it was still there.

"I'm wiped. That was a long day. How far did we go?" I asked, steeling myself for the answer. Steve told me we'd walked nine miles. "Really?" I asked. That was a new number. "Did we do nine miles on any other day so far?" I asked. Steve ran his finger down the list.

"Nope, it doesn't look like it. Except for that first day when we did 10.7," he said.

"That doesn't count," I said. "That was so flat it barely felt like exercise. Plus, our legs were so fresh." Hmmm, maybe we were getting stronger, albeit slowly.

Opposite the massive mountain, an airy open space was visible. We ate our dinner of freeze-dried beef stew with mixed vegetables, another favorite, then, when our legs didn't squawk so much at the notion of a few hundred yards of ambulation, we investigated the hole. We don't often get to look back at the scenery where our day's toil took place, but here was vivid evidence of our accomplishment. The small placid lake where we were camped emptied over immense glacier-polished slabs of granite plunging down to the valley we had traversed, taking the direct route near the switchbacks we had labored up. The sun was setting at the far end of the serene meadow, filling the broad canyon with saffron-tinged light—what a sight to behold.

A group of four middle-aged hikers sporting gray hair and well-used equipment was camped on this airy perch, and we spent some time exchanging pleasantries about the stunning view, the trail and trail gear—all popular topics for hiker talk. Steve got in a lengthy conversation about the benefits of hauling his camp chair all this way since one of the men had the exact same model. I was getting antsy since I wanted to lie down so I interjected saying, "We'd best get going. I want to turn in early so I'm ready for Muir Pass tomorrow. I've heard the trail goes on forever."

"It's not too bad," said one woman with curly hair and a friendly smile.

"Yeah, I'm really dreading the next one. I understand Mather is a bitch," I replied.

"I've heard Glen is worse," she said.

"I've got them both on my list of worries, but I have to go in order or I get overwhelmed." She laughed. "I get it."

I walked back to the tent with my stomach churning a bit with Muir Pass anxiety but reveled in enjoying the last rays of light shining on this special place. I re-read Ralph's account for the 9,000[th] time, reassuring myself that Muir was not the hardest pass, in his opinion. I tried to ignore the fact that Ralph's third day extended all the way from Mono Creek, where we met the 20 Milers, to beyond Muir Pass, a distance of just over forty-five miles. It was too outlandish to even wrap my head around.

Chapter 10: Muir Pass

We had barely walked twenty minutes toward Muir Pass the following morning when we heard the wump-wump-wump of helicopter rotors slicing through the cool early morning sky. I tried to focus my camera on the tiny speck, expecting it to stay high. Slowly it grew larger in my viewfinder. "I think it's going to land around here!" Steve said.

"What?" I said, ripping the camera from my face, "Where? There's not that much room between us and the lake." Watching it circle a couple of times, I said, "I think it's going to land right here in front of us!" We swiveled our heads back and forth, not seeing any other people or tents.

"I wonder what they're doing here. I don't see anyone around, "Steve said. We stood staring slack-jawed in amazement as the chopper landed directly across from us on a narrow strip of land between us and the lake. A tiny figure emerged from a clump of bushes that had obscured part of the lake shore. A brawny uniformed man with closely cropped brown hair leaned out of the helicopter and gestured emphatically, raising his outstretched hand and forcefully jerking it down to indicate that she should retreat so the chopper could power down safely.

We walked briskly down the trail and I said, "Hurry, let's see if it's someone we know. Maybe we can help."

Steve got a little ahead of me, calling over his shoulder, "It's The Texans!"

"Oh, no, what could be wrong?" I said, attempting unsuccessfully to jog with my thirty-pound pack on. We saw Jan first and I ran to her saying, "What's going on? What's wrong?"

Jim walked up saying, "It's me. I've been having trouble breathing the last couple of nights." I was gratified to see that he was up and walking around and relief flooded through me. Perhaps the situation wasn't dire but Jim's face looked drawn. Jan stood by, letting Jim tell the story.

He said, "I've felt sort of okay during the day, but at night I just couldn't catch my breath. We stayed here an extra night hoping it would get better, but I had another miserable night." I groaned silently. We had been so close, just on the other side of the lake, but this lobe of the lake was hidden so we hadn't even known it existed. "Some nice thru-hikers stopped earlier and used their satellite communicator to call for help. We relayed my symptoms to the ranger and to a doctor, and they called for a rescue."

By this time the parkmedic, a ranger with special medical training, had reached us. "Who's the patient?" he asked. I figured it was a good sign when the rescuers couldn't tell who the patient was in a group of four. We pointed at Jim and the parkmedic sat him down on a nearby boulder so he could evaluate him. I'm an RN, but knew better than to get involved. They know what they're doing, and they were in charge as soon as they were on the scene.

We turned our attention to Jan, saying, "Can we help with something?"

"Oh, no," she replied. "We've got it under control. Thank you, though. We'll be fine." I watched her tiny figure spinning around moving things randomly from this place to that and thought, *she's got to be hyped up on adrenaline and doesn't even know what she's saying.*

"We're not going anywhere until they've assessed Jim and have a plan," I announced, adding, "We're not leaving you alone here." Jan made a vague response, but I wasn't sure she was processing information very effectively.

A tall stout woman with russet colored hair slicked back into a tight ponytail emerged from the helicopter with a clipboard, saying, "I'm seeing a lot of stuff here, there and everywhere. What belongs to you?" She looked expectantly at Jan, who stared back uncomprehendingly. I explained that we weren't camped with them, so everything other than our packs was theirs. The woman's eyes got wider as she looked around disapprovingly.

"Don't worry, we'll get this all packed up. Just give us a few minutes," I said. Clipboard Lady turned away to walk back to the helicopter, her radio squawking. "Steve, can you take down the tent? I'll put all the food away. Jan, can you pack up your backpack?" We buzzed around, stuffing things into haphazard places in the packs, emptying water, packing up the food canisters and taking down the tent in record time. Jan started acting more like herself, laughing about the way we were packing up.

"Nothing is where it belongs, but that's ok. Who cares?" she said.

When Clipboard Lady came back she smiled, revealing some gaps where teeth had been, saying, "Okay, that's better. Now I have an idea of what we're dealing with." She exuded calmness and quietly asked Jan a few questions, including what she weighed with and without her pack. I noticed that Jim was alone, the parkmedic having walked back to the chopper presumably to confer with a doctor by radio at the base.

"How are you feeling?" I asked him.

"Okay. They don't know exactly what's going on, but he said my blood pressure is sky high." Tubing with nasal prongs delivered oxygen to him from a small tank. I suspected he was suffering from acute altitude sickness, which was unusual since they were well into their trip. "They said they might not be able to take Jan because of weight concerns," Jim said, looking worried. Jan was tiny and, in my opinion, probably weighed eighty pounds. Of all couples that could be stranded on the mountain, surely they could take this diminutive woman. "I guess I could refuse to go. I'm not leaving her out here," he said.

"Oh, that's not a good idea at all," I said, which made him look sharply at me.

"I won't do it. I won't leave her here," he said again, more stridently.

"All right, all right," I said, not wanting him to get agitated, "Let's wait and see what the final outcome is before we start jumping to conclusions." But already my mind was leaping to lots of conclusions. We would have to stay with Jan if they couldn't take her. I knew Steve would agree. All of a sudden the random way we had packed up all of the gear didn't seem like such a good idea. We might have to completely unpack everything to sort out what Jan would need. We'd have to get up and over Muir and Bishop passes, so that would probably mean at least one night if not two. Their tent would be needed as three people in our tent would be a bit too cozy. Our trip would be in jeopardy, but we could get back on the trail to do more of it even if it wasn't everything we planned. That would be okay—the trail would wait for us to return another time.

As it turned out, they did take Jan. Everything was packed up, stowed away and suddenly we were left in a swirl of dust, waving goodbye to our friends as they arced across the sky. There was nothing else to do but shoulder our packs and continue down the trail, feeling amped up and melancholy at the same time.

The rest of the morning passed in a blur. I barely noticed lake after beautiful lake, distracted by the events of the morning. The slog up to Muir Hut was exactly as promised, the longest ascent known to man. There was something about the relatively low angle, monotonous gray rock, lack of vegetation and that tiny beehive of a stone hut on the ridgeline that made this portion of the hike last a lifetime. I walked about a million of my ten-step cycles, so many that I had to start using different numbers. One to ten got really old, but twenty-one to thirty worked for a while. Muir Hut tantalized me shimmering like a mirage, never seeming to get bigger. Except that it did, eventually loom larger, and then we were there. At last!

We admired the handiwork of the Sierra Club, who built the charming, if ineffective, hut perched on Muir Pass (11,980 feet, 3651 m) that was supposed to protect hikers from the elements in this exposed section of trail. Apparently the walls and ceiling made from stacked rectangular stones leaked like a sieve from day one and was never the safest place to be in a lightning storm. Opening the wooden door, we let ourselves into the small, circular stone building and imagined how cozy it would feel back in the days when it was first built when fires would have been allowed in the fireplace. What a lot of work it must have been for volunteers to build the hut. As we exited the chilly cabin we shooed away the furry marmot guarding the hut and ate our lunch quickly. Then we were off, anxious to get this one behind us.

Over the rest of this day and the next, the descent into Le Conte Canyon was brutal, with lots of ankle-bending talus and steep steps built for seven-foot tall giants. We camped on a sliver of rock at Medium Lake—they must have started running out of creative naming energy to fall back on plain Jane names. Small Lake and Medium Lake, otherwise referred to as First and Second Unnamed Lake, is how they appear on the Tom Harrison maps. I couldn't get over this. With hundreds of backpackers each year, there's no name for two gorgeous lakes right on this popular trail? The one we camped at, Medium, a.k.a. Second, was one of my favorites, mostly for the squadrons of mountain yellow-legged frogs that leaped off sunny rocks to dive into the frigid waters of the deep lake every time we approached. I was extra-careful not to introduce any sunscreen or bug juice into the water, which can harm these sensitive creatures, by wiping down my skin away from the lake before washing up.

Steve chewed on his pencil as he tallied up our mileage. It had been a long day over Muir Pass, but I prepared myself for some wimpy number. I hated to ask but couldn't stop myself. "How far did we go?"

He looked up smiling. "Our biggest "real" day yet, nine and half miles. Even better than yesterday's nine miles." Woohoo! It was a small number compared to what I knew many others were doing. But this was our hike, and that was an incrementally large number for us.

I grinned and said, "Wow, two days in a row over nine miles. I can't tell because as we get stronger, the passes get bigger and it seems to negate our gains. But it's happening nonetheless. I would just love to know what kind of mileage we could turn in if we were snatched off this trail and dropped onto some magical flat trail at sea level."

"That's a good question," said Steve. "Maybe twelve or fifteen miles?"

I turned in, feeling satisfied with our day and our progress. We were staying on schedule and the miles were slipping away. Not only that, we were well past the halfway point.

I thought about The Texans and how their trip was cut short, and was glad I took extra photos of the parts they were going to miss. I hoped Jim was okay, and thought about what a different day it would have been for all of us if Jan had been with us. We would have gladly helped out, but the thought of having to camp at night with all of us worried about Jim and not knowing anything would have been tough. This was not an easy trail to hurry up on.

Chapter 11: Golden Staircase

Down, down, down we went, giving up our hard-earned altitude once again. We knew we'd have to make up the altitude tomorrow on the dreaded Golden Staircase. We were happy to see Grandma, who had caught up with us at lunch, and compared strategies for tackling the Golden Staircase. We both thought it would be good to break up the crux for Mather Pass, the hardest of the passes in Ralph's opinion, by doing the Staircase one day and Mather the next. I was curious to see what made Mather so bad. They all seemed hard to me, but I guessed that people thought it was difficult because most people did the two hard parts, the Staircase and Mather, on the same day.

A passing ranger asked us if we were thru-hikers, which pleased me for some reason. We were in an area with a lot of weekenders who came in through Bishop Pass and I wondered how she could tell—maybe our disheveled look or smaller packs. In general pack size goes something like this: Weekenders—huge, clean packs; JMTers—medium, well-worn packs; PCTers—tiny, battered packs. It appears that the longer the journey the smaller the pack size.

We camped one more night somewhere between the Middle Fork Trail Junction and Deer Meadow after yet another "niner," a 9.4-mile day, and enjoyed watching three does that spent the night and early morning within ten feet of our tent. We saw Grandma pass by, but she was trying to get even closer to the Staircase to be well-positioned for the hard walk the next day so we just waved as she took her slow, steady turtle steps.

We were no longer familiar with the low elevation ecosystems we were passing through. It was odd to see fern grottos and aspens. However, we could see the terrain opening up ahead. With my head down for the next few miles of easy loping, I fell into a reverie, forgetting the trail, thinking again about what my life would look like in a few years. I'd had snatches of these thoughts the last couple of weeks while hiking. But here, on this middling stretch of trail, it started crystalizing. I knew I wanted to spend more time outside, especially helping others to get closer to nature. In addition to my volunteer work in the state parks, I started formulating a plan to get more involved with the hiking community, focusing my writing on hiking and maybe even teaching backpacking classes. Who knows, perhaps I'd even write a book.

Deep in thought, I bumped into Steve's pack, realizing that he was speaking. "What did you say?" I asked, "Why are we stopping?" He stepped aside, still talking to someone else, I realized. It was a man leading a llama pack. We chatted for a few minutes, admired the regal creatures who were so much better suited to the trail than we were, then fell back to our trail pace. It would be nice to think that we took advantage of every moment in the Sierra to gaze at the scenery, but the truth was that we would probably bonk heads pretty hard with an oncoming hiker if both parties were similarly engaged in free-flowing contemplation of private thoughts. In fact, this is one of the benefits of long-distance hiking, when the trail becomes second-nature and the mind is free to wander, exploring the inner recesses that are all too often caught up in the structured world outside. I'm not surprised that some take to the trails to find themselves or heal emotional wounds, for what better place to do so than nature's sanctuaries?

We arrived at the foot of the 1,500-foot headwall of the Golden Staircase and I tilted my head up, all the wispy thoughts of the previous hours whisked away by the task at hand. It seemed impossible that there was a path. But indeed, there was. This was the very last section of the John Muir Trail to be constructed, in 1938, after the northern and southern sections were already built. I craned my head up and tipped it back, and it still appeared to be impossible. "Were they nuts?" I shouted over the roar of a nearby waterfall, the mist creating dancing rainbows in the sun. I began to detect a looping pattern off to the left as I squinted in the bright sunlight. Could that be it? I cursed Theodore Solomons who, as he gazed at these peaks while tending his uncle's cattle, had the crazy 14 year old's idea that there could be a path over the crest of the Sierra.

"Are you ready for Golden Staircase?" Steve asked, wanting to get on with it.

"As ready as I'll ever be. Let's get this over with," I responded. "Let's have a snack and some water and go for it." The day was uncomfortably warm, but it had to be done. We popped an energy gummy square and I resumed my plodding "pass" pace though this wasn't even a pass. The dry, rocky trail with the usual steps-built-for-giants gave way to lovely crimson and yellow paintbrush-filled tiny seeps in the cracks between frescos of colorful lichens glued to the granite—a wonderful distraction that lightened my mood. The higher we got the more ferns protruded from the side of the trail as seeps turned into small streams. I caught sight of movement up ahead. Something was in the ferns, but what was it? Out popped two grouse waddling up the trail, leading us on. We laughed, not expecting fowl this high up. That kept us entertained for a while, but eventually they darted off into the foliage, leaving us with nothing but more switchbacks. I could see Steve a couple of switchbacks higher than me, which made me groan to see how much elevation I had to gain in such a short distance.

I caught up to him at a stream where we splashed cool water on our faces. "How 'ya goin'? I asked, using the Aussie lingo we had picked up in previous travels.

"This is the hardest physical work I have ever done in my life," gasped Steve, strong words for a man who still treats scaffolding like a jungle gym and jackhammers concrete for fun. I hoped, once again, that we weren't in over our heads, but there was no choice but to continue on. *If we get through this, I'm never coming here again*, I thought, guiltily remembering how I had vowed to do the trail again with Laura. Maybe I'll hike to Red's, but never again will I see the Golden Staircase. Who would ever subject themselves to this craziness more than once? If Steve's heart would just hold up a little longer I promised myself we'd take it easy after this.

Finally, we got off the vertical wall and broke out into a jumbled amphitheater of sorts. We still seemed hemmed in by higher peaks and looking straight ahead we saw another seemingly impassable wall of rock. Knowing this was a difficult section I could imagine all sorts of crazy routes, but I had learned not to put too much stock in my first assessment of where the trail might be. Steve took a page from my usual playbook and threw himself on the ground, hat over his entire face, not moving a muscle.

"Are you okay?" I asked. This wasn't like him.

"Just... need...a minute," he said. A few minutes later he recovered enough to pick his way down to the gurgling creek and I fixed lunch—a tortilla with rehydrated black bean rice mix, corn, strips of string cheese and pumpkin seeds for crunch. I added some Tanka bites to mine for some extra protein and put some salami out for Steve to hack off. He came back looking a little refreshed, dripping water from his face. "That was a bitch," he said. We were beat, but we'd only been hiking for a few hours and wanted to get closer to the base of Mather Pass for the morrow.

After lunch we resumed hiking, appreciating the brief interlude of flat trail. We met a woman coming from the opposite direction. "Tell me there's a lake up there," I said, in a tone that might have verged a tiny bit into whining.

"Oh, yes, you're very close. Tell me about these, though. What are those for?" pointing at the four-inch covers on my pack straps.

"Those are my husband's invention. My collarbones protrude and I get wicked blisters from my straps. He had the idea of using sheepskin seatbelt covers, which come with Velcro closures, and cut them into short sections. They work great and it hardly cost anything," I said.

"What a great idea. I get those too but never thought of trying to pad them. I'm going to get some," she said. "But back to your question, there is a sneaky amount of gradual uphill to the second lake, which won't feel good. But the lakes are gorgeous. You have plenty of time, so just take it easy and you'll be there before you know it. You've already done the hard work."

I appreciated her upbeat, positive spin and she could probably see that the Golden Staircase had taken our mojo and stomped on it. Somewhat invigorated, we strode down the trail, thankfully bending away from the forbidding cliffs I had been looking at before. She was right. Palisade Lakes were stunning. Clear blue waters shimmered in the afternoon sun with small fingerling fish swarming at the shore. Now I could see the infamous Mather Pass, and it didn't look so bad. Maybe Ralph had just been having a bad day and it wasn't really the hardest pass. Not that I wanted to race up there today, but I was confident that by the next day we'd be up and over that puppy in no time. She was also right about the trail. When it started ascending again, our legs didn't want any part of it. But we made it to a crest before the big climb, which we would save until tomorrow.

A strange campsite, virtually split by the trail, spread out into two small clearings on either side. So much for the "no camping" rule within one hundred feet of a trail. I guess that falls into the "terrain permitting" provision, like a lot of lakeside campsites we had stayed in. "This would be okay if we were falling into camp at dusk, but I don't want to be in the middle of the trail with people tromping through all evening," I said. We searched around and I clambered up to a higher campsite. "Too small, but what's this?" I said, grabbing a blue package wedged into the bushes. "A Mountain House dinner—score!" I threw it down to Steve, whose eyes lit up.

"Cool. Extra food we didn't have to carry," he said.

"Let's go up a little further," I said.

"Okay," said Steve, "but not too far. I want to be close to the water and I don't want to go uphill much further."

"It doesn't seem like we're going to be able to get down to the lake as it's getting steeper. We don't want to get too far from that stream," I said, pointing at a cascade of water we had passed, tumbling down from a (presumably) higher lake. I climbed up the hill on the side of the trail and found two perfect, flat, sunny campsites on a huge plateau of flat rock. Double score!

We quickly set up camp. Steve pulled out his camp chair, sinking into it with a contented sigh. "That was a tough day, but our reward is this place. This must be one of the better sites we've had so far. We're going to have sun for a long time." We took advantage of the situation by taking turns bathing in the stream, Steve going so far as to stand in a short waterfall of freezing water to wash his hair while I did laundry in a lower pool using my zip-top bag to dump the water away from the stream. I soaked my burning feet in the cold, refreshing water and leaned back with the sun warming my face.

It was hard to resist obsessively staring at the wall of rock we had to ascend tomorrow. Mather Pass (12,100 feet, 3688 m), in the middle of Kings Canyon National Park, loomed ominously above our campsite. Hikers rhapsodize about the striking beauty of the high Sierra, but Mather wasn't beautiful. On the contrary, it resembled a slag heap of crumbling gray granite. Just then a whoosh of air startled me. Two black and white Clark's Nutcrackers fluttered and danced, swooping and diving together in an afternoon romp above the sparkling sapphire-blue water of Palisade Lake. We didn't see many birds up this high and I noticed that they didn't seem to be the least bit out of breath. Not like we were a few hours ago when we were struggling up the Golden Staircase.

I returned to camp, but there was no Steve. I scanned the flat rocks and spotted him lying face down on a hot rock like a lizard soaking up nature's warmth. He was a happy camper. Later, back in his chair he examined the new Mountain House meal. "Wait, it's already been opened," he said.

"Darn," I said. "I bet it's just trash. Instead of an extra meal, we'll be hauling out someone else's garbage." Suddenly our discovery wasn't so great.

"No, even better, it's a homemade snack pack," he said gleefully. "Look, it has some pita bread, sliced ham and some cheese."

"That's good, we can save it for an emergency," I said as he tore into it.

"Forget that, it's going to be my afternoon nosh," he said, stuffing his face with his newfound treat, demonstrating yet again the difference in how our brains work. "Besides, it won't last, the pita is already starting to fall apart," he noted. He did have a point. The ham certainly wouldn't be good for very long. It must have been left by a weekend hiker or it would have spoiled already. Nothing in the snack pack was anything I could eat on my migraine diet, so it had no appeal for me, much to his delight. My, my, he was having a most excellent afternoon—hair washing, snacking on unexpected treats and hot rocks, the Golden Staircase already fading into a distant memory.

After a dinner of a tasty cobbled-together meal of rehydrated sweet potato bark, ground beef and peas with a watery, but savory, reconstituted beef gravy, Steve pulled out a treat. We toasted each other with a shot of tequila as the sun slipped behind the peaks. "To us," I said. "That was well done. We conquered the Golden Staircase and we'll have Mather knocked out by noon tomorrow."

"Well before noon, I'd say," said Steve, as the fiery liquid burned our throats. "We only did 7.3 miles, but those were some of the hardest miles we've done so far, and we had a relaxing afternoon."

In the tent before bed, I scanned Ralph's notes again, even though I knew the words by heart: *Mather is the most difficult of the big passes.* I read the next part aloud to Steve. "The ascent is long, but most of the elevation is gained in short and shockingly steep bursts, including the infamous Golden Staircase. I started the day feeling strong, and (in retrospect) overconfident. I was mentally well prepared for the Staircase, and it felt easier than I had anticipated. But the undulating traverse of the Palisade Lakes seemed to go on forever, and when the final climb came, I realized that I had forgotten that the trail is extremely difficult, requiring not just cardiovascular effort, but rock hopping agility and strength. I pushed on up, but reached the top exhausted." Oh boy, if Ralph thought Mather was hard, I was in big trouble tomorrow. I was sure I'd feel just as weary as he had, even though we had already done the Golden Staircase and would be tackling Mather when we were fresh.

Chapter 12: Mather Pass

The next morning was chilly and a steaming mug of hot tea didn't faze the butterflies in my stomach as I stared up at the daunting pass. Mather was in such close proximity that I had studied every inch of the rock face and was anxious to get it over with. When we finally got on the trail, we found it to be well graded with a minimum of steps-made-for-giants. It didn't seem so bad and initially we were the only ones on the switchbacks. About half-way up I looked down and saw some brightly colored specks moving around. I thought I might keep my lead, but a couple of very strong hikers passed me. Steve pulled ahead too as I maintained my slow, steady pace. I reached a crest and looked down at a knot of people on the pass. Down?? Was it really necessary to throw in a little extra uphill before delivering us to the pass?

All of a sudden, Steve came running toward me, shouting, "Hurry up, you'll never guess who's here." I came out of my pass-induced reverie with a start.

"Who?" I asked breathlessly, related more to the thin air at 12,100 feet than to any sense of excitement or anticipation, though I was curious as to which of our friends we might have caught up to. I hurried across the flat ridge strewn with boulders that obscured different groups of people enjoying the view. Who could it be?

"Just hurry, you'll see," said Steve. I scanned the faces but didn't recognize anyone. I looked quizzically at Steve.

"Guess who that is," he said, pointing to a man sitting on a rock. I stared harder wondering if my hypoxic brain was giving out. Did I know this person?

"It's Ralph!" said Steve triumphantly. It took a couple of seconds for my brain to register the words.

"Ralph?" I squealed, "THE Ralph? The Ralph of JMT record fame?"

The slim, very fit man with close-cropped hair who didn't look his stated age of fifty, looked mildly bewildered, and said, "Yes, that's me."

"I can't believe it," I yelped, my voice still several octaves higher than normal. I threw down my pack and stood staring at him transfixed, completely oblivious of the dramatic views surrounding us. "Are you nuts? You've already done the JMT twice this year, and broken the speed record, and now you're out here for a THIRD time? Can you not get enough of this place?" I asked.

"Well, actually this time I'm doing the Sierra High Route," he replied unpretentiously.

"You're kidding? You're going cross-country now?" I said. This was too much. I could barely take it all in. "Does it share part of the trail with the JMT? I thought it was all trail-less." I asked.

"I think we're sharing the trail for this bit across the pass, but I'm not quite sure for how long," he replied, "I think it's just a short distance."

"Where did you come from?" I asked.

"When you get down to that first lake, look up and to your right. Look for the most ridiculous route possible. That's where we came down," he said, shaking his head.

"Are you doing it with your friend here?" I asked, looking at a bemused guy sitting next to Ralph.

"I ran into Seth out there, and since we seemed to have compatible styles, we decided to do some of the trail together." I was blown away. I already regarded Ralph as being the rock star of the JMT, but here he was performing additional audacious feats.

"What's next after this incredible summer?" I asked.

He got a faraway look in his eye. "I don't know, I don't have anything planned," he said. "But the yo-yo record is pretty soft..." I couldn't remember what a yo-yo was in my addled state, but he explained that it's a round trip—hike from one end to the other, then turn around and hike back. "I wonder if I could maintain my pace from the earlier trip this year. Going NOBO (northbound) is easier," he said.

I took his photo with Seth, and then asked if I could get one with him. I posed with the famous Ralph, as giddy as if I were with a rock star. "Are you in the JMT Yahoo Group?" he asked. I replied affirmatively. "Me, too," he said.

"Yes, I know, that's how I knew about your record," I said. He asked what my Yahoo name was and I said, "It's my real name, Inga Aksamit."

"Oh yes, I know who you are," said Ralph. Wow, the rock star knew me! I promised him I'd send him the link to my blog post and, with that, he and Seth gathered their packs and faded down the gravel ramp, on to more crazy exploits.

In the meantime, Steve had gotten involved talking with two girls from South Carolina, Michelle, who went by the trail name, Brownie, and Sarah. Their legs looked sturdy with hiking muscles toned and taut. Baseball caps shaded their faces and long sleeves protected their arms from the intense Sierra sun. Waist-long brown braids gave Sarah a girlish look though both looked like they couldn't have been more than 30. She sported red running shorts while Brownie, whose hair was captured in a ponytail, wore a hiking skirt. They were telling an amusing story about two young guys who were doing the whole trail with nothing but huge jars of peanut butter and Nutella. That's it—no crackers, tortillas, bread or anything. Just a spoon and a gigantic thick mass of nut butter. Steve had seen the big jars in the hiker barrels at MTR and wondered who would ever think of carrying anything that heavy. But if that's the only food you're carrying, it's probably a decent calorie to gram ratio. The other distinctive thing about them was that they both carried bongs. Sarah said, "What, they don't know how to roll a joint? They have to carry a *bong* with them on the trail?"

"And not just one bong, but *two*? I guess they aren't ultra-light," I said.

"They're nice guys though, and they laugh at themselves," Sarah said.

Later, I asked Steve how he knew it was Ralph on the pass. "Some people at the top were saying how hard Mather was, along with the Golden Staircase, and I told them there was a guy who had done the whole trail in four and a half days," said Steve.

Ralph had looked up, startled, and said, "I'm that guy. I'm Ralph." What are the odds that we would run into the (JMT) world famous Ralph, and not only that, to know it was him? It would have been all too easy for us to have hung out on the pass right next to him and never have known it was him. Most of the conversations we'd had on the trail didn't result in name exchanges, so this meeting was a minor miracle. I was so glad we hadn't missed the opportunity to meet him and grateful that Steve had come to get me.

After that much excitement, I could barely settle down to eat a snack of protein-rich energy bar. I was equally elated to see that it was only 11:15 a.m. We knocked out one of the worst passes before lunch. But because we had already conquered the Golden Staircase, it wasn't nearly as difficult as we had anticipated. I was on a natural high between meeting Ralph and achieving a big milestone. Muir Pass was but a distant memory, Donahue Pass felt like a lifetime ago, and one by one we were ticking off the big passes.

I floated down the trail on a cushion of adrenaline and tried to pick out the notch that Ralph had described, but the whole ridge looked ridiculous. I couldn't see how anyone could have come down any part of it.

We put in a respectable 8.4 miles through a barren basin, stopping at the South Fork of the Kings River. We chose a secluded campsite nestled under fragrant pine trees. An added attraction was a fern-fringed creek bubbling merrily by, serenading us as we dined on freeze-dried beef stroganoff. It wasn't a Ralph-day in terms of mileage, but meeting Ralph himself was even better. We were happy to have put the dreaded Mather behind us and to have hiked a decent number of miles. Maybe we were finally, at long last, getting trail hardened.

Chapter 13: Pinchot Pass

Shouldering our packs the next morning, we looked forward to an easy half-day with no passes. After crossing the river, we spotted some sunglasses on the trail with a note containing a name. "That's odd," I said. It seemed improbable that someone had recognized sunglasses and knew that the owner was behind them. After pondering the mystery for a few minutes, we left them there untouched and loped along the moderately angled trail.

Marjorie Lake was our destination. We planned to spend the afternoon there, hanging out in the afternoon in lieu of a full zero day. Once again, however, I found that once we reached the lake there was nothing appealing about spending an afternoon and night in this inhospitable place. After walking through many beguiling spots in the morning, we had begun ascending and standing at the lake at 11,050 feet above tree line, I confronted the truth: I'm a tree person. The whole way along the trail, my favorite places were those that had a mix of trees and living things. According to Wenk, who has a PhD in Integrative Biology, the area that I favor is known as the upper montane zone, which exists at 6,500 to 9,000-10,000 feet in the Sierra. She described this area in detail in our guidebook. It is here that white firs, red firs, western white pines, Jeffrey pines, western junipers and lodgepole pine, *lots* of lodgepole, flourish. Even the subalpine zone at 10,000 feet to treeline is okay, where whitebark pines and lodgepole pines somehow find a foothold in the shallow, sandy soils. It's the alpine zone above tree-line, where we now stood, that leaves me cold. Yes, the grasses, sedges and wildflowers are quite pretty up close. But from afar, this landscape can look quite barren and bleak. Many, perhaps even most, people describe the southern half of the JMT as being their favorite, and the place they most desire to return to. But I found much of it to be austere and lonely. It was dramatic and powerful, to be sure, but it didn't beckon me to want to sit down and stare at stark rock walls, or a scene that looked like tailings from a mining operation, all afternoon. It's heresy, I know.

"What do you think?" Steve asked. "This is where we planned to camp and we can take the afternoon off. Does that sound good?"

"Ummmm. I don't know. This doesn't look like a cozy place to camp. And I don't feel that tired, do you?" I responded. "If you're tired we can stay, but I think I'd rather press on," I added. Wait, was that my voice? Volunteering to add more miles to the day? That didn't sound like the same person that was on the beginning part of the hike.

"Okay, I'm game," said Steve. "Let's just check the mileage and I'll figure out somewhere else to camp. I don't want to commit us to a huge number of miles today," he said. After some consultation with the maps, it looked like we could camp below Pinchot Pass, not too far below the top. "There's only one campsite though, so we'll have to see if someone is already there, or if there is room for us."

Off we went, clicking off another pass. It wasn't easy, of course, but relative to passes like Muir and Mather, it was a cinch, with a well-graded trail and only a half a million switchbacks. Pinchot is almost the same elevation as Mather, at 12,130 feet (3697 m), but it was only about 1,200 feet from our low spot that morning. I stepped off the trail for a short time to let two long mule trains go past, the long ears of the mules contrasting with the perky ears of the muscular horses in the lead. A cowboy straight out of a Marlboro commercial with a ten-gallon hat, leather chaps and well-worn boots led each lead horse as it was too steep to ride. Five sure-footed mules with heavy loads of equipment and supplies for trail crews were tied together in a long line behind each horse. Near the summit, I paused again to appreciate the colorful murals on the rock created by yellow map and orange firedot lichens with their distinctive mosaic patterns resembling continents and brains respectively. As much as the overall landscape was infertile to me, these little splashes of color could be found in all sorts of nooks and crannies. I just needed to narrow my field of vision to find the beauty.

At the top, a few people were huddled into their jackets against the brisk wind, and there was none of the lively chatter that we'd had at Mather. Even the marmot, scouting around for snacks, barely elicited more than a quiet reach for the camera. While we were eating lunch, Steve looked over at two sturdy young men in their early twenties eating peanut butter out of a jar with a spoon, their scruffy beards and long hair blowing in the wind. All of a sudden something clicked in his brain. "Wait a minute, are you the Nutella boys?" They looked over, grinning.

"Yeah, that must be us," one said, holding up a large jar of Nutella that matched the bucket of peanut butter they were eating.

"We heard about you," exclaimed Steve, "Did you leave a big jar of Nutella in the hiker barrels at MTR?"

"Yeah, we over-planned so we had to leave that behind. How did you know it was us?" one of the young men asked.

"For one, it's kind of obvious. No one carries that kind of weight on the trail. But we talked to two women who told us your story," said Steve.

"Oh, it must have been Sarah and Michelle," one said.

"Yes, the Carolina girls," said Steve.

"Yeah, those are the girls. They were so nice. They even left me these sunglasses because they knew I lost mine," one said. Aha, that explained the sunglasses with the note. The girls had found the sunglasses and knew the Nutella Boys were following behind. I loved how the trail was becoming interconnected, but in a different way compared to our little community in the second section. Here we were creating a web of seemingly disconnected vignettes that actually linked us together into a trail community. We might never see some people again, as opposed to leapfrogging back and forth with the same people like we did in the middle of the trail.

"We saw those sunglasses and couldn't figure out the story," I said.

"Yes, and I'm so grateful to them. My eyes thank them," he said, his fair skin glistening in the high altitude sunshine, his face as red as a tomato.

"Let's see, I think they said something about a bong?" I asked, wondering if they'd be embarrassed. Heck no, they lit up like a Christmas tree.

"Yes, it's right here," one said, reaching over to his pack, where a bong was prominently lashed to the front, in plain view.

"Did I hear that you both have one?" I asked.

"Yep, here's mine," said the other, pulling out an intricate looking carved wooden pipe.

"Did you really need two?" I asked.

"Sure, why not. They don't weigh much," came the reply. "I'm glad you brought that up. I'm going to have a nice toke right after lunch," he said. Ah, the simple pleasures of youth.

"Can I get your picture with the peanut butter and Nutella?" I asked. They jumped up and grabbed the buckets of nut butters. I jokingly said, "Maybe the bong, too?"

"Oh, yes, definitely, great idea," said one boy, reaching for the bong.

"Maybe just the peanut butter and Nutella," I said, thinking better of it for their sake. But they insisted, posing proudly with big smiles. So I snapped the photo of two beaming young men, just graduated from high school, who were having a dreamy adventure of a lifetime before entering the real world of college, jobs and responsibility.

We camped just below Pinchot by a small lake. Though it was in the alpine zone, which has now been identified as my least favorite terrain, it was a pleasing place. The delicate ecology was very apparent at 11,500 feet (3505 m) and I enjoyed scrutinizing the tiny plants and flowers that managed to find a foothold at this inhospitable elevation. The blue, delicately veined Sierra gentian held its long trumpet toward the sky, rising above the drab gray-green sedges and I tried to avoid crushing any living thing as I walked around.

By now our set-up was pretty predictable. We set our packs down, I scouted around to see if there was a better campsite than the first one spotted and then we made our decision. It was probably too close to the lake to meet leave-no-trace principles but had clearly been used before so, rather than crush more fragile plants, we set up our tent on a compacted sandy site. Steve unfurled our homemade Tyvek footprint and laid it on the ground. We took opposite ends of the tent and carefully placed it on the Tyvek. Grabbing the ends of the unwieldy center pole we snapped them into place, fastened the clips on the sides and staked out the edges. This took all of about a minute and a half. I left Steve to puff air into his sleeping pad and set up his sleeping bag because two of us rummaging around in the tent at the same time got annoying. After filling our Nalgene bottles with water at the lake, I waved the SteriPEN around in the water until the flashing green lights indicated it was purified. I unloaded the food onto my pack cover, having found that it could be useful as a clean pantry instead of being dead weight when it wasn't raining. After Steve had his gear organized I threw my stuff in the tent, tucking my camera, glasses and phone into the small pocket. I set up my sleeping pad and bag next to Steve's and laid out my evening wear, comprised of long pants, wool socks and a long sleeved T-shirt. I blew ten breaths into my sleeping pad, almost passed out from the effort in thin air, recovered and repeated until it was fully inflated. After a short break, I blew up my inflatable pillow, a luxury that was worth the extra 1.6 ounces. The sun streamed into the tent turning it into an overheated sauna. Instead of crawling out, I stretched out on my pad and luxuriated in the warmth, letting my overworked muscles and psyche unwind, drifting off in an exhausted slumber.

I awoke from my nap feeling sweaty, grimy and ready to get clean. Searching for a private spot to wash up, I found the perfect secluded lake lined with big flat slabs of granite on the shallow bottom. I loved not having mud squishing between my toes and the weak sun was enough to warm the crystal clear water—so much so that I got in up to my waist, a novel experience for this cold-water wimp.

I saw an airy blank space beyond the lake and wondered what was there. After my bath, I walked to the other side of my soaking tub, becoming almost disoriented by the other-worldly sight of a large lake far below. Stunted trees dotted the shore while a cluster of small islands rose from the center and I could picture hobbits and gnomes settling happily there. Protected by high walls of granite, the lake was calm and serene. I sat for a long time soaking up the view, feeling at peace, grateful that this special place had been revealed to me. Seeing the scattered trees, which stood like sentinels guarding the gates of a hiker's Valhalla, reinforced my appreciation of living things. Happy and content, I skipped back to our campsite bubbling over with enthusiasm for the special places I had discovered.

"You've got to come and see this wonderful swimming hole I found," I said to Steve.

"Really? I'm pretty happy right here," he said with a questioning lilt.

"Yes. You can't miss it. You'll feel so good if you get in. Bring your towel," I said emphatically. He looked reluctant for a moment, then got up slowly and ambled over to the tent. He picked up his sliver of a camp towel.

"Okay, show me this special place," he said. I grabbed his hand.

"Let's go, before the sun goes down." I dragged him over the scree. When we got to the lake I turned to him and said, "See, is this not the most perfect spot to take a dip?"

"It's pretty nice," he said with a smile, proceeding to the edge. Eventually he lowered his body into the lake, enjoying the firm surface below his feet as much as I did. After he dried off we sat in the sun, soaking up the warm rays and talking about our day.

"How many miles did we do today?" I asked.

"We hiked 6.8 miles today, which was more than we planned," Steve said.

"That's pretty decent, considering that we were going to have a nero," I said. A nero is like a zero day, but a few miles are hiked. "And we knocked off another milestone, Pinchot Pass. I'd say that was a pretty good day." I showed him the other lake, which didn't inspire him as much as the swimming hole. Oh well, maybe he couldn't be expected to see the fantastic creatures that filled my imagination. We walked back to our tent as the sun dropped behind a peak, suffusing the multicolored rock into a rich tapestry of crimson, ochre, copper and burnt orange. My legs felt strong and I looked forward to the next day, which looked to be mostly downhill. It was nice to feel like I was finally getting used to the trail, a contrast to the first days when I felt like it would never happen.

Chapter 14: Dollar Lake

We woke shivering to the distressing sight of a thick, white layer of frost icing everything, even the inside of our tent. We both refused to consider getting out of our down womb until the sun was shining directly onto our tent. Not until the tiny plants around us had given up their sparkling sheen to the solar effects of the sun and our tent had absorbed all the residual water it had accumulated did we deign to emerge, shaking the last of the ice crystals from our camp shoes that we had left outside.

I was a little off. I had a headache, felt fuzzy and a wave of nausea passed over me shortly after breakfast. Could I still be suffering from the effects of altitude, even after three weeks? Or, worse, was this a harbinger of another migraine coming on? I was disgusted with my physiology. Just when I was feeling robust my body showed its weakness again.

After drying everything off and drinking lots of tea to warm up and try to clear my head, we took off. I felt grateful that the whole morning was spent traveling downhill. It would have been trouble if we'd had a pass to ascend that day. Luckily it was a relatively easy stretch, so I just rolled along, counting the hours until I could get back in the tent. It wasn't pleasant, but at least there were no twinkling lights inside my head.

I was dragging, fatigue making each step a chore. I could barely take in the sights, but noticed the broad, polished rock bottom of Wood's Creek on my left. Water glided down the steady gradient like a giant aquatic-park slide, brilliant sunlight shimmering on the smooth surface. I envisioned lying in the cool water, feet first, arms crossed over my chest, floating down to the next junction. Now that would make this so-called easy day effortless. It was a nice fantasy, but I knew the water was frigid, not cool, and that the gentle slope would inevitably plunge into rocky falls and I'd be broken into a thousand pieces. I kept plodding.

We pulled into the Wood's Creek junction at lunchtime, but not without crossing one more JMT landmark—the bouncy suspension bridge crossing the creek, known as the "Golden Gate of the Sierra." Steve loves these bridges and bounded across gleefully. I did not love them and was grateful for the sign proclaiming, "One person at a time on bridge," so Steve wouldn't be compelled to give it an extra bounce on my behalf. The photo of me looks typical—head down, staring intently at the slats (many of which were missing), clinging to the cables as I watched the rushing water churning below my feet.

At a large clearing on the other side, I flung my pack down and sat down heavily. "I'm glad that's over," I said.

"Don't forget we still have more, and it's a little uphill," said Steve.

"Ugh," I groaned, "I forgot." Busying myself with getting lunch together, I barely registered the presence of a few other people. I was still in a daze of fatigue. But gradually I tuned in to a family with a young child and a couple of young women. When I could place my attention on something other than myself, the scene before me suddenly came into focus. "Are you doing the JMT with your kid?" I asked.

"No," came the reply from the mom. "We're just doing a five-day loop over Glen Pass. We didn't want to push it with a two-year-old." Who cares if it was only five days—to do any backpacking with a two-year-old was inspiring. Plus, this was one of the most notorious passes.

"Wow, I'm impressed," I said. It turned out that little Sage, who was happily crawling all over her dad, had been on all kinds of adventures in her short life with her active parents, a type of lifestyle that is all too rare. Hiking, biking, sailing, surfing, skiing, rock climbing—this kid had done it all.

Elizabeth, Sage's mom, asked what was in my plastic cups. I explained that it was a Tabbouleh mix that I had added water to in the morning, and now it was rehydrated and ready to eat in our tortilla with a little string cheese. The two young women joined in the conversation, one of them saying she was a farmer in South Carolina.

Steve woke from whatever reverie he was in, saying, "Wait, you're the Carolina girls. We talked to you on Mather."

"Oh, wow," I said. "You know the Bong Boys. We ran into them on Pinchot and we knew exactly who they were." The girls started laughing and we shared a giggle.

"The one guy found the sunglasses you left for him and he was so happy," I said.

"Those boys... They weren't the most prepared. But that's great that he found the glasses. I was so worried about his eyes," she said with a slightly motherly tone. The magic network of trail connections continued. "Hey, do you want an orange?"

Huh? An orange? In the middle of nowhere after three weeks on the trail? I tried to process this information in my head, which was still a bit sluggish.

"Did you carry an orange all this way?" I asked.

"We got a resupply here, and the guy from the pack station brought all kinds of fruit as a treat. We didn't even know we'd be getting it. I'm such a fresh fruit person from living on a farm that I ate three pieces already. But I can only eat so much at once," said the farmer girl.

"Sure, I'll take an orange," I said, trying to act casual. Who would turn down fresh fruit at this stage of the journey? She brought it over, dropping the sweet orb in my hand. It could just as well have been made of pure gold for its value to me.

I tried not to look voracious, but she said, "Don't worry, nectarine juice was dripping down my chin when I was trying to talk to the packer, but I just couldn't stop." I stripped the skin, carefully divided the treasure into two perfectly even pieces and reluctantly handed half to Steve. I peeled one section off and closed my eyes briefly as the succulent citrus juice dribbled down my throat. Heaven, pure heaven. All conversation came to a halt while I devoted myself to the task at hand.

I felt revived after all that animated conversation, not to mention the delectable fruit, and busily packed up as we said a round of goodbyes to our new friends. Taking off at a good clip, I hoped that brief high would carry me through the afternoon. However, as soon as the trail started gaining elevation, I slumped again. I dragged up the last part of the trail, knowing that it was important to get as far as we could to be positioned for the dreaded Glen Pass the next day. Struggling with a complete lack of energy, I sat on a rock and let the emotion wash over me.

This was the moment I had always known would come. The lowest emotional point on the trail presented itself to me in the high country around Rae Lakes. I had nothing more to give. I was spent. I didn't want to be there anymore, I was tired of the trail, and I wanted to be somewhere else, anywhere else. What was that thought about doing the trail again with Laura? Forget it, I was done, never again. My chest heaved—were those tears sliding down my cheeks?

I heard the drone of a fighter jet overhead. With a start, I remembered the daily missions that accompanied us on the High Sierra Trail a couple of years prior. Fighter pilots from Edwards Air Force Base had become our constant companions on that trail as they buzzed the high country in an endless loop. The memory of a major melt down I'd had at Wallace Creek on that trip, right when we met up with the JMT, made me chuckle. It had been a similar day where we had had an easy morning and then had to ascend and, like today, my body had simply rebelled. I had sat on a rock on the top of a hill we had climbed and cried big heaving sobs. Right then a jet flew over, so close I could see the pilot. I had waved and thought about what a baby I was being. I had chosen my adventure and was doing it for fun but what that pilot was training for was serious. Though I suspected he might be having some fun buzzing the high peaks.

I was cheered to hear the jet now because it made me realize that we were nearing the end. We had walked so far that we were actually in the Southern Sierra, in the range of Edwards Air Force Base. Still, the growing sense of satisfaction didn't replace my desire to be transported anywhere off this trail.

I looked up and saw a slender, handsome young man with fine features and long, blond dreadlocks approaching. *He's probably full of cheer and thinking nothing of whipping out twenty miles going uphill every day*, I thought. I surreptitiously wiped my eyes and pulled myself together. "Hi, how 'ya doin'?" I said in my best happy voice.

He stopped, looked at me, then looked up at the steep walls on either side of us. "I want to be done. I'm so ready for this to be done," he said, looking significantly less cheery than I had imagined. In fact, he looked completely dejected.

"Me, too! I'm with you. I don't know what is going on, but this is my worst day on the trail and I'm ready for it to be over. How many days have you been out?" I asked.

"Eleven days," he said. Eleven days—that was hardly anything in comparison to our twenty-one days on the trail.

"I miss my dog. And my girlfriend," he said. I'm sure she appreciated being included, even if she came in second. "Do you have anyone at home?" he asked, "Kids or anything?"

"No, my husband is up ahead. Well, I have my parents and friends at home, but my husband is my trail partner," I said. "Could you tell him I'm okay, just taking a short break? He'll be worried about me because he knows I'm having a bad day," I said.

"Sure," he said. "*Are* you okay?"

"Oh, yes. I just have no energy. But I don't think we have much more to do, so I'll be fine. Hang in there," I said. He trudged on.

I sat quietly for a few more minutes, thinking about how hard it must be to feel so lonely and sad while hiking solo. I shrugged into my pack, mulling over the fact that I was the luckiest girl in the world to have a husband who was here with me. So many people on the trail had spouses and partners who didn't like to hike. But here I was, living this adventure with my friend and partner for life. It was time to buck up and get up there to him. The conflicting emotions ricocheted around my head. I only walked a few minutes and found Steve lounging on a downed tree. "Hi. Did that guy tell you I was taking a break?" I asked.

"Yes, he did. Are you okay?" he asked, looking concerned.

"Yeah, but things don't seem to be improving. No energy. I'll be all right, though. I know we have to get to Rae Lakes, so I'll just take breaks when I need to. I can be tough," I said.

"I've been looking at the map and I think we can stop earlier and it'll still be okay tomorrow," he said. That made me brighten up considerably.

"Yay. That would be great," I said. We walked literally five more minutes to a small lake fronting a dramatic rock formation shaped like a fin, called Fin Dome. All in all, I had probably walked 10 whole minutes since my near-meltdown.

"This is it—Dollar Lake," he said.

"Thank you, honey, this is perfect," I said, smiling. The day was saved. "I hate to say it, but I'm kind of done. If I could possibly walk out tomorrow, I would. But I don't think I have two high passes in a day in me. I swear, if I could push the button on the SPOT and have a concierge helicopter come and get me, I'd do it," I said.

"I'm right there with you," said Steve. "This is a long time to be on the trail."

"I wonder if we're in some kind of weird vortex, where everyone who passes a certain point is zapped with an emotional slump," I said. At least we were on the same page so I didn't feel bad about bringing him down.

I dove into the tent as soon as it was set up and fell into a deep sleep for about an hour, awakening to the happy sounds of Sage "helping" her parents set up camp. I poked my head out of the tent to announce to Steve that I was temporarily revitalized.

Elizabeth saw me and came over. "Do you have a scalpel?" A scalpel? That didn't sound good. No one had ever asked me for a scalpel before. I made a mental note to put a scalpel in my first aid kit.

"No, what do you need a scalpel for?" I asked. I was hoping she would say she needed to cut a strap off of her backpack. But if I had thought about it, that would have made no sense. Just about every backpacker carries a knife for those sorts of events.

"I fell in that little creek on the way up and a big stick rammed in my leg. It's pretty deep, so I thought if I had a scalpel I could slice into my leg and grab the end with tweezers. I can feel it, but I can't get to the end. It's so weird, it doesn't hurt at all." Yikes, this was one tough girl, this slender woman with her blond hair pulled back in a ponytail who looked like she could be a model.

"I'm kind of glad I don't have one so we don't have to do surgery," I said, making a mental note to leave the scalpel out of the first aid kit. I looked at the wound, which showed an outline of a twig under her skin, and we talked about strategies using the tweezers. She walked back to her tent. I thought about it awhile and went back to her. "You don't want to do surgery out here. They are probably going to have to make an incision the entire length of the splinter. If it's in that deep it won't be easy to pull out. If you can get out in a day or two that would be better."

"Yeah, we can cut our trip short if we have to. I was really hoping to spend the full five days out here, but if we have to get out early we can make that happen." She had a good first aid kit with alcohol swabs, antibiotic ointment and bandages, so she was prepared.

It looked like I wasn't the only person having a bad day, which didn't make me feel any better. One of the Carolina Girls had skinned her knee pretty badly so Neosporin was making the rounds. Everyone was nursing their trail wounds, physical or emotional, that night. Maybe the meltdown vortex included minor trail injuries. Better to get it out of the way before Glen Pass.

Chapter 15: Final Passes

I woke up feeling normal. Better than normal, I felt full of verve and vitality as if I'd had a day or two off. Who knows, maybe I was so tired the day before that my body got a restful sleep. Or, more likely, sleeping at 9,288 feet instead of 11,000 feet allowed my body to get the deep slumber I needed. I felt positively giddy with energy. I thought of Glen Pass, looming in the distance. *Bring it on*, I thought to myself. I'm ready!

Elizabeth reported that her leg hurt a bit. She was going to check at the ranger station on the way to Glen to see if they had any supplies. Sage was a chatterbox, pausing at a sign in front of the lake that listed closed sections, "reading" it to her mother, "Mommy, look, it says this way to the hotel and Jacuzzi." We all laughed, wishing it was true. Apparently Sage's adventures had included fancy hotels with spas. We bid them goodbye, hoping that we'd see them again, but knowing that we probably wouldn't.

After a few pleasant hours of easy hiking past stunning Rae Lakes—yet another string of high alpine lakes framed with improbably dramatic peaks—we did pass Elizabeth, Peter and Sage. They had stopped to get water, and we waved at them as we began a moderate ascent. It looked like we were topping out, but I knew we couldn't have made it to the summit so easily. Nothing is that easy in the High Sierra. We climbed up the last bit of the false summit and stood facing another seemingly impenetrable wall of rubble, so implausible that I laughed out loud. "You have to be kidding. It's not even possible that there is a trail on that thing." I tried my squinty-look technique to see if I could pick out even a fragment of a trail. Nothing. Just a muddled heap of loose rock. On the summit, I thought I could see a tiny speck moving around. I figured that must be Glen Pass (11,970 feet, 3648 m). From that place, I scanned right and left just below the ridge. Wait, was that a faint horizontal line going off to the left? I turned my attention to the hodgepodge tumbling down from that direction. "Ohhhh, I think the switchbacks are way over there," I said.

"Maybe," said Steve doubtfully.

Off we went, gearing down for the big ascent. Steve was walking at this usual pace, but for some reason I was nipping at his heels. That was a first; I always lagged far behind on pass ascents. I kept wishing I could pass him or make him speed up so I could get this over with but settled down into his rhythm. He slowed down even more, his breathing labored. "Are you okay?" I asked. He gasped for air and mumbled something. Uh oh, it was his turn to have a bad day. In one day, we had flip-flopped. I was thankful, once again, that we took turns. I don't know what we would have done if we both had a bad day at the same time— maybe we'd just sit down on the trail and refuse to move, like the Dog People's black labs.

158

"This thing is kicking my butt," he said.

"Okay," I said, "We know how to do this. One step at a time and we're not breaking any speed records. Let's stop and catch our breath." I looked down to see Elizabeth popping over the top of the false summit. I figured they would catch up to us, but I hoped it would be a little wider than where we stood now so they could get around us safely with the baby carrier. Steve started walking as the trail sashayed back and forth in an all-too-familiar pattern. On a particularly narrow part of the trail, I could sense the family gaining on us, and I could tell Steve was still dragging. As we rounded a switchback, I saw a wider space with a couple of boulders we could sit on. "Let's sit over here and wait for them to pass," I said. Steve had a slightly unfocused look so I just pointed at the rock and said, "Sit." He sat. I could hear Sage singing in her carrier.

They passed us with cheerful greetings, after which Steve said, "I can't believe I was passed by a guy carrying a *baby*. How embarrassing."

I laughed. "Well, for one thing, he's about thirty years younger than you, and for another, you're not having your best day on the trail." Steve dredged up some energy and we continued our laborious trek. I felt strong all the way to the top but was not prepared for what I saw—hundreds of feet of nothingness over the other side. *Whoa,* I thought to myself, *don't look down there.* Casting my eyes on the other side wasn't that much better. All of the other passes had had broad, flat tops where people could mill around, sit down and have a snack. This one was a true knife edge with a narrow trail along the top for a few hundred feet before plunging down again on the other side. Well, maybe it was a dull knife edge since it was plenty wide enough to walk on.

Sage was out of her carrier, running around making me nervous. But Elizabeth had a close eye on her. Steve was partially obscured by a clump of boulders and I couldn't see beyond him. Looking back, he said, "Guess who's up here?" I knew it wasn't Ralph—he was probably in Yosemite Valley by now.

"Grandma?" I asked.

"Yep."

There she was, looking fresh and energetic with nary a complaint about the trail. She was entertaining another Japanese couple, talking about her trip to Annapurna, a seventy-fifth birthday present to herself six years ago. Elizabeth came over to meet her and we all took photos of her with Sage, two to 81, celebrating the vast spectrum of ages enjoying the trail.

The descent from Glen Pass was one of the most treacherous yet, with loose scree on tight switchbacks winding down to a sapphire blue lake surrounded by bleak gray rock. We had thought we might camp at one of the small lakes just below the pass, but decided, once again, that it was too inhospitable. So we pressed on. Steve had rallied a bit, but by the time we had walked two more miles he was sagging again. I felt bad because I knew we had

160

stopped early yesterday to accommodate my bad day, which had made this one even longer. We progressed to Charlotte Lake, a large body of water we could see below us for quite a while. Even from a distance I could tell a lot of people were camped there with brightly colored tents. When we arrived, tents lined up one after the other making the narrow shoreline look like a suburban development. We scouted around, finally finding a spot high above the lake on the less populous side just as the sun slid behind a nearby peak. We quickly got our camp chores done as a damp chill descended upon the lake. I tried to do as much as I could to relieve Steve so he could collapse. I got dinner started and filled large dry bags full of water from the lake so we wouldn't have to clamber up and down the hill so much.

As I kneaded the freezer bag filled with warm water and dehydrated marinara sauce, I thought about Ralph. When he broke the southbound JMT record, at this point he had been on the trail only four days compared to our twenty-two. That was an unbelievable difference, and yet we each hiked our own hike to achieve different ends. I was proud of our effort and felt almost as trail hardened as I had hoped. My legs felt strong and I had a lot more stamina that when we started, even if we weren't pulling huge miles. Steve and I were in sync, experiencing the highs and lows of the trail together, supporting each other through tough times and celebrating our successes. The times of quiet reflection had centered me, making me appreciate the natural wonders that have been protected for us in our parks and forests.

That night it got really cold, and we weren't surprised to wake up to frost. Sometime in the night, I had given my down jacket to Steve so he could put it over his torso in his sleeping bag. I knew he needed to get some sleep after his difficult day.

The moisture from the lake had coated everything with sparkling ice crystals. When we emerged from our tent we appreciated our location, positioned to receive the earliest warming rays of sunshine. We shivered for a while, but my heart sang with glee—it was the last day. I knew that I would wish I were back on the trail within a few days, but all I had wanted for two days, and especially at this moment, was to be off the trail. Only one more pass and we were done! It was almost incomprehensible to think that tonight this would all be behind us. Steve was feeling like his old self, so we packed up and were raring to go before people on the crowded side of the lake even stirred.

After walking a mile up to the four-way junction in a moonscape of sandy flats, I stared at the sign. It pointed the way to Forester Pass, the next pass on the JMT, but also to Kearsarge Pass, our way out. The sign said it was only seven and a half miles to Onion Valley, also known as civilization. It was almost more than I could take, but it wasn't over yet. There was one more pass to drag myself over, passing a gaggle of gorgeous lakes that barely piqued my interest. I'd had enough of amazing alpine wonders. The only thing I wanted to see was a hotel, shower and restaurant, in that order. With its wide, loping switchbacks, the three-mile ascent to Kearsage Pass was easy. However, I wasn't as spry as I had been on Glen. It was only fitting that the last ascent would be as laborious as the first.

I looked back in the direction of the JMT and felt a slight pang that we'd be missing Forester Pass. But I wasn't the slightest bit disappointed to miss a repeat of Whitney. Once was enough for that mountain.

When, at last, I reached the top of Kearsarge Pass, I threw down my pack and hugged the waiting Steve. "We did it, we did it!" I exclaimed, jumping up and down. "I never thought it would end but we're here." He had a big smile on his face, too. Then I went and hugged the Kearsarge Pass sign. I briefly touched my face to the cold metal while I closed my eyes and gave thanks that there was no more uphill.

"You did a great job. I'm glad that's over," said Steve. I danced over to him and gave him another hug.

"We were a great team," I said.

A couple who had resupplied came up from Onion Valley. When they heard that this was our planned exit, they high-fived us enthusiastically and congratulated us warmly. It was a nice gesture to commemorate our finish, and I got a little teary, then jubilant that it was over.

But it wasn't quite finished. That was the last pass, but we still had four and a half miles of descent, with a long, long time to appreciate the surreal view of the alkali flats of

Owen's Valley. Time slowed to a crawl. The faster I walked, the longer the trail stretched out.

"The trail will never end. We think the finish line is down there, but the trail will snake across the valley, crawl up into the Inyo Mountains and pretty soon we'll cross the Great Basin and end up in Kansas. We'll be like Forrest Gump, criss-crossing the country forever," I said. Okay, so maybe I was getting a little petulant. Steve just laughed.

Suddenly it really was over. There were no more steps to take. The trail simply ended in a paved parking lot in Onion Valley. There was no finish line, no trumpet announcing our arrival and no trophy. There was just the satisfaction that we accomplished our goal and walked a long distance.

We called our shuttle driver and were lucky that he could come and get us. We were a full day early, but he said he could squeeze us in. We spent the hours waiting for him in the lee of a concrete outhouse which provided the only shade in the blazing heat. Once we finally reached Mammoth Lakes, the first meal, shower and night in a real bed were as luxurious as I had dreamed. Over a massive steak dinner with creamy mashed potatoes and crisp green salad dripping with Italian dressing, we reminisced over the highs and lows we experienced. Steve's heart attack almost derailed the whole trip, while my adventure started off inauspiciously with a migraine. Exhaustion and altitude wreaked havoc with our planning at times. Yet the people we met brought the trail to life, including Ralph, our constant companion, our cohesive group in the middle and the string of connections we made at the end. The journey was hard at times, but worth it for the sense of accomplishment we gained in the splendor of the High Sierra.

With berry pie and vanilla ice cream dripping down my chin, I said, "So when we do Forester Pass, I was thinking we could go NOBO from Cottonwood Pass and come out over Kearsarge Pass like we just did today. That way we could pick up the one missing pass and still avoid doing Whitney a second time." Steve looked at me with dismay. "I'm not doing that," he said, "I'm never going up that pass again." But I knew he would.

Chapter 16: Bonus Chapter-Mt. Whitney

Two years before we hiked the John Muir Trail we pondered whether we were up for such a long trek. High up on Alta Peak in Sequoia National Park one weekend we gazed at the jumble of craggy mountains forming the nearly impenetrable Great Western Divide. Steve surprised me by saying, "We could come back next month and do the High Sierra Trail."

"That's something to think about. Those 72 miles would give us a good taste of whether we're ready to bite off the whole JMT," I said, barely breathing, hoping he wouldn't dismiss the idea.

It stuck. The next thing I knew it was a month later and we were toiling through some of the most ruggedly beautiful terrain the Southern Sierra has to offer. Day Six found us at Wallace Creek, having had the spiky Kaweah Peaks as our constant companions for days. As we joined the JMT, I noticed an immediate uptick in the numbers of hikers on the trail, most of them with heads bent down. They were making their miles after clearing ten high passes, with only one more major milestone, the mighty Mt. Whitney. We had had our share of ups and downs, too, and were eagerly anticipating standing on the summit of the tallest point in the continental United States.

As soon as we arrived at Crabtree Meadow, where we had planned to camp, a debate ensued. "I think we should stay here. There's less risk of lightning and we've been getting storms every afternoon," I said. Crabtree Meadow was a lovely grassy spot ringed with trees and a burbling creek nearby.

"Yeah, but if we go to Guitar Lake we'll be that much closer to Whitney and it'll make tomorrow a lot easier," Steve said. His logic ultimately prevailed. He was feeling strong, but I straggled up the last couple of miles to the bleak, treeless campsite at Guitar Lake and hunkered down next to a large boulder. We were unprepared for the tent city filled with throngs of hikers congregating on the windy slope in preparation for the next day's assault. We had seen few people on the High Sierra Trail, but we went with the flow. Gazing at a particularly ominous looking peak for a long time, we took selfies in front of it and memorized the features, psyching ourselves up for the thought of tackling that monster the next day. Then we consulted a map and realized it wasn't even Mt. Whitney. We were basically right under the massif, but couldn't get far enough away to see the top. So much for planning.

While filtering water at a stream, I struck up a conversation with an older woman doing laundry in a collapsible bucket. "Are you doing the JMT?" I asked.

"Yes, and I can't wait for it to be over." I didn't know what to say. I wasn't expecting that response. I had thought that the JMT hikers would be so trail hardened by this point that they'd want to stay on the trail forever. "It was harder than I was anticipating and I just want to be off the trail," she continued. "I'm doing it with my son and he's so much stronger and has a schedule he needs to adhere to, so the pace was more than I could handle. I can't get ahead of it and I'm getting more run-down each day." I felt for her, watching her slowly rinse and wring her clothes out. She looked like she was on the verge of tears.

"Just think how great it will feel to stand on top of Mt. Whitney," I said, trying to lift her spirits. "It's your last big obstacle."

"Oh, I'm not going to summit. I'm going up to Trail Crest and over the other side. I have no desire to go to the top." I tried to encourage her to stick with it, but she was adamant—she just wanted out and nothing was going to stop her. She was going to split off from her son at Trail Crest; he would continue to the top while she planned to head straight down to the end of the trail. I felt sad for her and realized there was nothing I could say to change her mind.

I was tired myself, and nervous about the next day. We ate dinner early and turned in shortly after dusk. Just as I was dozing off I heard the familiar drone of the fighter pilots from Edwards Air Force Base. Night training began and I anticipated the runs overhead as the pilots flew loops around Whitney, the hum barely audible at first, gaining in intensity until the crescendo built directly overhead. Then the Doppler effect waned, only to repeat ten minutes later. I sighed and got into the familiar rhythm. Every day we had observed or heard these training missions at various times of the day and night, juxtaposing the advanced technology against the craggy wilderness. The pilots headed home and quiet was restored at 10 o'clock. Headlamps switched off across the plateau as hikers burrowed into their sleeping bags.

Awakening seemingly moments later to the muffled sounds of camps being broken down in the pitch black, I looked at my watch—it was 3 o'clock in the morning. I poked my head out of the tent and saw faint bobbing lights from headlamps already toiling up the trail. Not us. I snuggled back into my sleeping bag and blotted out the noise. We rose at 8 a.m., had a leisurely breakfast and started up the well-worn track an hour later. The ascent to the top was prolonged and steep with many switchbacks and the air was noticeably thinner above 13,000 feet (3963 m). Taking our time we stopped frequently, even if just for a few moments, to catch our breath. When we got to Trail Crest we started co-mingling with the flow of day hikers coming up from the east side. Looking neat and clean, some in flimsy shoes and sweatshirts, their appearance was very different from thru-hikers.

We had considered staying at the top overnight to see the purported stunning sunrise, but before we even reached the summit we were both thoroughly chilled.

Though we had enough clothes it wasn't appealing in the least to stay on the windswept jumble of rocks. Besides, I had a headache, was nauseated and my eyes were puffy from the effects of the rarefied air and all I wanted to do was get up, and then down as quickly as possible.

The view from Mt. Whitney was undeniably spectacular, and we spent a few minutes just soaking it all in. I saw the friendly Kaweahs to the west that had looked over us during our entire trip—this would be the last we would see of them for a very long time after we dropped over the other side. The dry, high desert of the Owens Valley stretched out to the east before bumping into the Inyo Mountains, while the jumbled masses of Sierra peaks marched north and south. They beckoned us to continue, but not today. The broad summit of Whitney itself was scattered with huge slabs of granite that resembled giant building blocks.

We were lucky that the weather cooperated. Threatening gray clouds hung over us, but the raindrops held off. The clouds seemed close enough to touch and at 14,505 feet (4421 m) it wasn't that much of a stretch. They truly weren't that far away. The small weather station, ubiquitous in photos of the summit, bristled with lightning rods. With its metal roof, it was no place I wanted to be in a storm though the thought of potential shelter was tempting.

We signed the register and were touched to see a notation that a couple had gotten engaged on the PCT the day before. Romance had bloomed on the trail like the wildflowers we saw all the way to the top. I had never been much of a peak bagger, but it was satisfying to add my name to legions of people who summit the pinnacle each year.

After the initial excitement wore off I curled up between a couple of blocky boulders with happy summiters all around me and took a nap. Steve patiently tried to start a high-altitude fire in our wood-fired camp stove with some twigs he carried from lower elevations. His persistence paid off and soon the kettle was boiling. I had no appetite, another effect of the altitude, but I forced down some warm, nourishing split pea soup.

When we headed down the infamous 100 switchbacks to Trail Camp on the eastern side it didn't seem so bad and it appeared that we would be down before we knew it. Alas, it was an optical illusion. It's true what they say. The switchbacks do eventually seem endless and you wonder if you will ever finish. A couple of sections were pretty tricky with a heavily eroded trail at the very top, so much so that I carefully planted my pole on the downhill side before swinging over it. After more than 60 miles of hiking, this was the sketchiest segment we had encountered. It was a reflection of the impact of the 25,000 hikers that pound this part of the track every year.

It was about 6 p.m. before we finally made it down to Trail Camp, the first camp on the eastern side of the Sierra, in a flat plateau next to a large pond. It was another tent city, with a mixture of people coming down and others preparing to go up the next day. It was a long but rewarding day and I was only too happy to set up the tent, eat a quick meal and drop into my sleeping bag.

We were awakened by muted booms in the distance. It was an eerie sight to see twinkling stars in the inky night sky above but to look down on lightning illuminating the thick, puffy rain cloud far below in Lone Pine. It was like watching a movie from behind the screen and reminded me of what the inside of my head looks like during a migraine. I counted the seconds before the bursts of thunder, tracking the storm until it was directly overhead. Lightning flashed all around us as I held my breath, waiting for it to head toward the top of the mountain. I was exceedingly happy that I was not on the summit of Whitney at that moment.

I wasn't excited about using the Wag Bag, a NASA-designed receptacle to hold human waste which contained cleverly named Poo Powder. The ranger had bestowed it upon me in Sequoia National Park when we picked up our permit. After hauling the dead weight across 72 miles for use only in the Whitney Zone, I still hoped to avoid using it. After seeing the disturbing amount of toilet paper and poorly disguised burial sites of mounds of poop on rocks covered with only the thinnest layer of vegetation, however, I decided that it was for the best. There were simply too many people in this high impact zone for the meager soil to absorb that much human waste so I did my part to mitigate filth. The Poo Powder turned the solid matter into a gel and odor neutralizers took care of any bad smells.

On our last day, we went down, down, down, and intermittent rain drops drove us even faster. I couldn't help but stare at some of the day hikers in tank tops and shorts scrambling to unfurl their flimsy $2 ponchos when the hail rained down and the wind whipped through the narrow canyon. I saw a man carrying a bear canister in his bare hands. That just couldn't be comfortable all day. After a couple of hours of rain, we passed a guy who looked miserably soaked to the bone, his saturated cotton sweatshirt hanging to his knees.

I interrogated everyone we passed about the status of food, but many had started hiking in the wee hours and hadn't been to the Whitney Portal Store. Then, however, I started hearing tantalizing tales.

"I hear the hiker's breakfast is killer."

"My wife said they used to have great hamburgers."

Hamburgers! Burgers are not usually at the top of my wish list, but I became obsessed. I could taste the charred meat, the doughy bread, maybe a tomato and lettuce. With ketchup, plenty of ketchup. I fantasized about French fries. We had considered staying another night on the flanks of the mountain since we were a day early before our pick-up, but I quickly discarded that plan—burgers were at the finish line. And when we got there and bit into the giant hamburger it was everything I dreamed of and more because the real French fries cut from potatoes on-site were irresistible and the huge chunk of fresh lettuce and thick juicy tomato on the grilled meat were heavenly.

We sated ourselves and rested but had to put off a hot shower. There were none available at Whitney Portal and our ride wasn't due to pick us up until the next day. We enjoyed chatting with hikers going up and coming down and had more rounds of burgers and beer. I relished our last night sleeping under the stars at the Whitney Portal Hiker's Campground.

When our friend, Cindy, arrived with coolers loaded with an array of delectable fresh treats and chilled Chardonnay we said our goodbyes to the mountain. I mentally saluted the brave men and women who protect our country as they screamed overhead in their fighter jets, by now feeling an affinity for our steady companions as they accompanied us on our ambitious adventure.

That night, over huge platters of elk and duck at Season's Restaurant in Lone Pine, we regaled Cindy with trail stories of our eight days traversing the Sierra, which she patiently listened to long after her interest wore out. I looked at Steve and said, "Well, what do you think? Are we ready for the JMT?"

"Definitely, we're ready. Time to start planning," he replied.

Epilogue

I didn't think that skipping the first and last sections would bother me in the least, but I found that they nagged at me. Though we had hiked Half Dome and Mt. Whitney in the past there were little sections that my feet had never been on. The next summer we took an Ansel Adams Gallery photography workshop in Yosemite and tacked on an overnight trip from Tuolumne Meadows to Happy Isles, knocking off that section quickly. Chase and Laura came with us and we started from the exact spot that we began our trek the previous year, but turned around and went the opposite direction. We climbed more uphill than expected, traveled past comely Cathedral Lakes where Laura took a swim, and somberly walked through the blackened remnants of the Sunrise Fire. Finally, we were absorbed into the madness of Yosemite Valley where we were mixed and churned with the crush of tourists.

Of course, Steve caved immediately and helped plan the last section we had missed, which was basically just Forester Pass. Still not wanting to climb Mt. Whitney again, we planned a path further south, originating at Horseshoe Meadows. The fifty-mile hike would take us six days to go north to Kearsarge Pass, just as I had proposed during our celebratory dinner. Unfortunately, the dry conditions resulting from our four-year drought led to big fires and the huge Rough Fire nixed our plans. Undaunted, we will try again next year and then it will be well and truly done.

With the passage of time, the friends we met along the way are still major highlights in our memory banks. It has been most enjoyable to keep in touch through Facebook and email, celebrating life's achievements and sharing the down times. Kevin, the bubbly young man we met at Red's, did a semester abroad in Thailand, making good on his promise to travel more. Melody graduated from medical school and she and Gabe get up to the Sierra whenever they can. Jim quickly recovered from HAPE and he and Jan are traveling the world from their home base in Texas. Little Sage moved with her parents to Dubai and was spotted climbing mountains in Nepal. Her mom, Elizabeth, did end up needing surgery to remove the large splinter and I was thankful a real doctor did it under sterile conditions. Brownie is working on her next book and has been a supportive fellow author. I still keep in touch with Ralph and followed his attempt at breaking the NOBO record this year, thwarted by a respiratory issue (see my article, "Ralph Burgess sets SoBo John Muir Trail record," with his trip report about establishing the SOBO record that I read so often on our hike at *IngasAdventures.com*). Everyone is continuing to have their own adventures in one way or another.

My trail-inspired idea to teach backpacking classes came to fruition through the support of John Roney, the

Park Manager at Sugarloaf Ridge State Park, where I volunteer. He gave me free reign to design and execute a class. I'm going through training now to become a Sierra Club hike leader so I can lead classes in the mountains that I love so much.

We have a lot more hiking goals to achieve and all we need is time. The clock is ticking so we're busy planning our hikes for next year and beyond.

Appendix A: Gear List

The Basics

Backpack (49-Liter REI Flash 52)
Sleeping bag (Sierra Designs Backcountry Bed)
Sleeping pad (Thermarest NeoAir)
Tent (Sierra Designs Lightning 2UL)*
Trekking poles
Trowel/toilet paper/wipes/small bottle of hand sanitizer
First aid kit

Clothing

Synthetic, odor-control, quick-dry short sleeve shirt (1)
Synthetic, odor-control, quick-dry long sleeve shirt (1)
Synthetic, quick-dry hiking pants (REI)
Synthetic, quick-dry hiking shorts (Cloudveil)
Ultralight down jacket (Uniqlo)
Raincoat (Sierra Designs UL Trench)
Rain pants (REI)
Thin liner gloves
Socks (Injinji toe socks-1 pr)
Socks (Tilley travel socks-1 pr)
Socks (Fit wool socks-1 pr)
Underwear (ExOfficio Give-N-Go-2 pr)
Fleece beanie
Hat (Tilley)
Bandana (wash cloth)
Camp towel

Hiking boots (Merrell Moab Ventilator)
Camp shoes (Teva flip flops)

Kitchen

Camp stove (JetBoil Flash)*
Mug (GSI insulated mug-2)
Spoons (MSR long handled folding spoons-2)*
Bowls (REI polypropylene bowls-2)*
Multitool (Leatherman Micra)
Bear canister (Garcia)
Hydration bladder (3-Liter Camelbak)
Water bottle (1-Liter Nalgene)

Electronics

Android Phone (Inga) with apps for reading, listening to
podcasts, note-taking, GPS location check, Guthook's JMT
app
Kindle Paperwhite (Steve)*
Solar charger (Bushnell Solarwrap Mini) with cord and wall
charger
Earbuds (for podcasts)
Satellite messenger (SPOT Gen 3)
Camera (Canon SX130 IS)
Headlamp (Black Diamond)
Water Purifer (SteriPEN)*

Carried by Steve

Notes on Gear

Steve and I shared some equipment. He carried most of the "kitchen" equipment while I carried the bear canister with most of the food. We couldn't fit all the food into one canister for the last section, which was 10 days, so Steve carried a second canister. For the first half he packed some clothing and loose items in it until we needed it for overflow food from our resupply at Muir Trail Ranch.

When compiling my list of gear I focused on what was necessary for survival (including the Ten Essentials), to adhere to Leave No Trace principles and to make the trip comfortable and enjoyable without adding much weight.

I didn't bring anything that I didn't need and didn't discard anything along the way. I was very glad that I brought rain gear with all the precipitation we had and wore my rain pants several times as an extra warm layer even when it wasn't raining. The only changes I would have made is that next time I'd bring my warmer fleece-lined wool hat (Tuck's Tooque) instead of my lightweight fleece beanie and a pair of lightweight long johns as it was very cold (upper 20s F) a couple of nights.

My base weight was about 18 pounds without consumables such as food and water. When we were fully packed with food and water both of our packs were about 25 pounds for the first two legs. This increased to 35 pounds for me and 40 pounds for Steve when we faced the ten-day stretch, which is probably the maximum we could do without a resupply. We'll probably continue to replace some of our older gear with lighter weight models as time goes one. My old, heavy Garcia bear canister, in particular, is due for a replacement. I have a 7-ounce Ursack that I use where legal, but it is currently not approved for Yosemite, Sequoia or Kings Canyon National Parks.

This is not a complete list but touches on the highlights. To see a complete description see the "What's in my pack?" series of articles or my gear list in Backpacking Resources on my blog, *IngasAdventures.com*. There is also a detailed list of my first aid kit contents on the Backpacking Resources page.

Appendix B: Meal Planning

Meal planning was a time-consuming process that seemed to go on forever. My main concerns were to provide nutritious food that would fuel us without excessive weight loss over three weeks of strenuous hiking and have enough variety that we could eat it without gagging. With the valuable resources and files provided by the knowledgeable people on the John Muir Trail Yahoo Group I was able to look at examples of other meal plans, find formulas for calculating protein and calorie needs and create my own strategy.

I created some quick-and-dirty spreadsheets to examine the calorie and protein content of our usual backpacking diet, compared that to recommended values and found that our protein level of about 40 grams per day was inadequate. Forty grams a day is okay for a weekend, but we needed closer to 60-70 grams a day to maintain our muscle strength over the long haul. My easy solution was to provide one energy bar per day that contained 20 grams of protein. I also boosted our protein by adding extra freeze-dried meat to Mountain House meals, dehydrated some of our own dinners with plenty of meat and added nuts, flax and chia seeds to our daily oatmeal. It was pretty easy to get to about 2,300 calories a day. Steve lost seven pounds and I lost three pounds, which wasn't bad, all things considered.

The following represents some of the foods we ate on the trail.

Breakfast

Granola
Instant oatmeal
Extras: freeze-dried berries, chopped hazelnuts, flax seeds, chia seeds
Powdered full-fat milk
Tang orange drink
Tea

Lunch

Tortillas stuffed with variations of the following:
Dehydrated beans (black, pinto, or white), rehydrated on the trail
Tabbouleh mix
Corn soup mix
Tanka Bites
Salami
String cheese
Dehydrated spicy salsa
Pumpkin seeds
Freeze-dried corn

Dinner

Mountain House freeze-dried dinners
Home dehydrated meals such as Asian stir-fry, pasta with marinara sauce, jambalaya, stew

Snacks

Energy bars
Jelly Bellies
Lemon Drops
Mixed Nuts
Chocolate
Jerky

Drinks

Crystal Light
Tang
Hot chocolate
Electrolyte replacement powdered drink

There is an article, "Meal Planning for the John Muir Trail," on my blog, *IngasAdventures.com*, where I review ten foods that worked, five that didn't and additional details about our meal planning.

Appendix C: Keeping Clean

I don't like feeling grimy so the only way I could go days on end wearing the same clothes is to maintain good hygiene. It's also important to keep clean to prevent illness. I keep a small bottle of hand sanitizer in our toilet kit and wash my hands with soap and water before preparing dinner.

To bathe, I sit by a lake or stream but don't scrub down in the water. I dip a sturdy gallon-size zip-top bag into the water, saturate a bandana and wipe myself down, one area at a time. I start with my face, then wash my arms, torso, legs and groin. I usually don't use soap, which has to be rinsed and causes environmental degradation. I keep dipping my washcloth in my bag, then discard the dirty water 100-200 feet from the lake or stream. This prevents any sunscreen, insect repellent or other chemicals from contaminating the water. Sierra water is generally way too cold for me to submerge myself, though many others have a stronger constitution. If, however, it's an invitingly warm day I will then go for a swim or walk in up to my knees. I also bring a small supply of wet wipes for a quick wash-up on those evenings when I'm too tired to go through my usual routine, the weather is bad or I'm in a place where there is no privacy. To wash my hair, I fill a one-liter bottle with warm water and lather up away from the water source. Many will think this is overkill, but it keeps me sane and comfortable on the trail if I'm clean.

I do laundry every day or so. After I wash myself I fill the zip-top bag with water and add a couple of drops of bleach, add my clothes and let it soak for fifteen minutes. I discard the water away from the water source, rinse and hang to dry on a length of paracord we carry for emergencies. At a minimum, I try to wash my socks and underwear every day but if I'm exhausted or it's pouring down rain I might go two days or more. If we have an easy day and it's a bright, sunny afternoon I wash our shirts as well.

I use a "pee rag" after urinating, instead of toilet paper. Urine is nearly sterile and in most environments my thin quarter of a bandana dries quickly dangling on the back of my pack. It gets washed every day, along with my socks and underwear. I learned about this from ladies on a backpacking forum and found that lots of women use a pee rag. As long as I'm talking about personal hygiene I'll mention that I use "dehydrated" wet wipes instead of toilet paper in my toilet kit for Number Two and place them in an opaque bag to pack out.

My article, "Doing Laundry on the Backpacking Trail," has more information about washing clothes at *IngasAdventures.com*.

Appendix D: John Muir Trail Itinerary

Day 1: Lyell Canyon Trailhead (Tuolumne Meadows, Yosemite) to Ireland-Evelyn Trail Junction

Day 2: Ireland-Evelyn Trail Junction to Rush Creek (over Donohue Pass)

Day 3: Rush Creek to lake near Garnet Lake (over Island Pass)

Day 4: Garnet Lake to Johnston Meadow

Day 5: Johnston Meadow to Red's Meadow Resort

Day 6: Red's Meadow Resort to Red Cones

Day 7: Red Cones to Duck Pass Junction

Day 8: Duck Pass Junction to Fish Creek

Day 9: Fish Creek to Mono Creek Junction (over Silver Pass)

Day 10: Mono Creek Junction to Bear Creek

Day 11: Bear Creek to Sallie Keyes Lake (over Selden Pass)

Day 12: Sallie Keyes Lake to Muir Trail Ranch

Day 13: Muir Trail Ranch (zero day)

Day 14: Muir Trail Ranch to Goddard Canyon Junction

Day 15: Goddard Canyon Junction to Evolution Lake

Day 16: Evolution Lake to Medium Lake (over Muir Pass)

Day 17: Medium Lake to LeConte Canyon

Day 18: LeConte Canyon to Upper Palisades Lake

Day 19: Upper Palisades Lake to South Fork Kings River Junction (over Mather Pass)

Day 20: South Fork Kings River Junction to lake below Pinchot Pass (over Pinchot Pass)

Day 21: Below Pinchot Pass to Dollar Lake

Day 22: Dollar Lake to Charlotte Lake (over Glen Pass)

Day 23: Charlotte Lake to Onion Valley (over Kearsarge Pass)

Appendix E: High Sierra Trail Itinerary

Day 1: Crescent Meadow (Sequoia National Park) to Buck Canyon

Day 2: Buck Canyon to Precipice Lake

Day 3: Precipice Lake to Sky Parlor Meadow

Day 4: Sky Parlor Meadow to Kern Hot Springs

Day 5: Kern Hot Springs to Wallace Creek (JMT junction)

Day 6: Wallace Creek to Guitar Lake

Day 7: Guitar Lake to Trail Camp (via Mt. Whitney)

Day 8: Trail Camp to Whitney Portal

Appendix F: JMT Pass Elevations

Trail Begins-Happy Isles		4040 feet (1231 meters)
Pass 1	Cathedral Pass	9700 feet (2957 meters)
Pass 2	Donohue Pass	11060 feet (3371 meters)
Pass 3	Island Pass	10200 feet (3109 meters)
Pass 4	Silver Pass	10740 feet (3274 meters)
Pass 5	Selden Pass	10900 feet (3322 meters)
Pass 6	Muir Pass	11980 feet (3652 meters)
Pass 7	Mather Pass	12100 feet (3688 meters)
Pass 8	Pinchot Pass	12130 feet (3697 meters)
Pass 9	Glen Pass	11970 feet (3648 meters)
Pass 10 Forester Pass		13110 feet (3995 meters)
Trail Ends-Mt. Whitney		14505 feet (4421 meters)
Trail Exit-Whitney Portal		8330 feet (2538 meters)

Source: Wenk, Elizabeth, *John Muir Trail, The Essential Guide to Hiking America's Most Famous Trail*, 5th Edition, Wilderness Press, 2014.

Appendix G: Recommended Reading

Guidebooks:

Rippel Raymond, *Planning Your Thru-Hike of the John Muir Trail e-book*, available at JMTbook.com. Good for early planning.

Wenk, Elizabeth, *John Muir Trail: The Essential Guide to Hiking America's Most Famous Trail, 5th Ed.* Wilderness Press, 2014. Good for detailed planning and for reading on the trail to prepare for the next day.

Maps:

Asorson, Erik, *Erik the Black's John Muir Trail Atlas, 2nd Edition*, Blackwood's Press

Harrison, Tom, *John Muir Trail Map-Pack*, available at www.TomHarrisonmaps.com and Amazon

Parks, K. Scott ("Postholer"), John Muir Trail Southbound, Scale: 1:63,360, available for free download at www.postholer.com

Website:

Pacific Crest Trail Association website, John Muir Trail section (www.pcta.com)

Hiker Forums

- John Muir Trail Group in Yahoo Groups (www.yahoo.com)
- John Muir Trail Facebook Group (www.facebook.com)
- Ladies of the JMT Facebook Group (www.facebook.com)

About the Author

Inga Aksamit is a Northern California travel writer whose passion is adventure and exploration. She loves nature so she gets out whenever she can to hike, backpack, ski, mountain bike and paddle. The west coast of the Americas, the far north and all around the Pacific Rim are her favorite destinations. She's been backpacking for about 15 years, volunteers at local state parks, teaches backpacking classes and leads trips for the Sierra Club. She and her husband, Steve, split their time between their home base in Sonoma County, California and Lake Tahoe in the Sierra.

Publications include "Bear Encounters on the Chilkoot Trail" in *Travel Stories from Around the Globe*, "Rolling Down the River" in *Coast and Kayak Magazine*, "Upside Down in Western Australia" in *Journeys: On the Road & Off the Map*. Her blog, Inga's Adventures (www.IngasAdventures.com), is loaded with backpacking tips, trip reports and other resources.

Thank You for Reading

If you enjoyed this book, please write a short review on Amazon. Your feedback is valuable to me.

To see a slideshow of our trek go to ingasadventures.com/book/.

To contact me or follow my adventures, see my blog, IngasAdventures.com. I'd love to hear from you and am happy to answer any questions.

I am active on several Facebook Groups, including John Muir Trail, Ladies of the JMT and California Backpacking Women. My Facebook Author Page is Inga's Adventures.

Follow me on Twitter, @IngaAksamit.